The Church in the Latin Fathers

The Church in the Latin Fathers

Unity in Charity

James K. Lee

LEXINGTON BOOKS/FORTRESS ACADEMIC
Lanham • Boulder • New York • London

Published by Lexington Books/Fortress Academic
Lexington Books is an imprint of The Rowman & Littlefield Publishing Group, Inc.
4501 Forbes Boulevard, Suite 200, Lanham, Maryland 20706
www.rowman.com

6 Tinworth Street, London SE11 5AL

Copyright © 2020 by The Rowman & Littlefield Publishing Group, Inc.

All rights reserved. No part of this book may be reproduced in any form or by any electronic or mechanical means, including information storage and retrieval systems, without written permission from the publisher, except by a reviewer who may quote passages in a review.

British Library Cataloguing in Publication Information Available

Library of Congress Cataloging-in-Publication Data Available

ISBN 978-1-9787-0687-3 (cloth)
ISBN 978-1-9787-0689-7 (pbk)
ISBN 978-1-9787-0688-0 (electronic)

Contents

Acknowledgments	vii
Abbreviations	ix
Introduction	1
1 Tertullian of Carthage	13
2 Cyprian of Carthage	41
3 Augustine of Hippo	59
4 Leo the Great	91
Conclusion	107
Bibliography	115
Index	119
About the Author	123

Acknowledgments

Many friends and colleagues have provided faithful support in order to bring this work to completion. I would like to thank John C. Cavadini, John Sehorn, Abbot Austin Murphy, O.S.B., Bruce Marshall, Billy Abraham, Steve Long, Craig Hill, Evelyn Parker, Simon Kim, Steve Rankin, Denise DuPont, Matthew Wilson, Ben Voth, Phil Carlson, Matthew Esquivel, José Santana, David Moser, William Glass, Roy Heller, and Pamela Hogan. I am grateful for a Sam Taylor Fellowship in 2016 from the General Board of Higher Education and Ministry of the United Methodist Church, and for a University Research Council Grant in 2017 from Southern Methodist University, which supported the research for this project. Many thanks to Neil Elliott, Mike Gibson, and the great team at Lexington/Fortress Academic.

My wonderful wife, Anna, has been a constant source of love, joy, and encouragement. This book could not have been completed without her. Thank you, I love you. I would also like to thank my family and friends for their steadfast support, especially Young Lee, Edward Lee, Hugh and Terry Burnstad, Ben and Nora Vodila, Mara Burnstad, the Cavadini family, and the Slonkosky family.

In loving memory, I give thanks for the beautiful witness and friendship of John Paul "Casey" Slonkosky, born July 15, 1955, entered into eternal life on June 21, 2019. *Requiem aeternam dona ei, Domine, et lux perpetua luceat ei. Requiescat in pace. Amen.*

This book is dedicated to my daughter, Mary Margaret Anne Lee, born May 29, 2017, with love and gratitude, as ever.

Abbreviations

Series and Collections

ANF	Ante-Nicene Fathers
CCSL	*Corpus Christianorum Series Latina*
CSEL	*Corpus Scriptorum Ecclesiasticorum Latinorum*
LG	*Lumen Gentium*
NPNF	Nicene and Post-Nicene Fathers
PL	*Patrologia Latina*
RSV	Holy Bible, Revised Standard Version
WSA	The Works of Saint Augustine

Augustine

Agon.	*De agone christiano* (CSEL 41:101–138)
Bapt.	*De baptismo contra Donatistas* (CSEL 51:145–375)
Catech.	*De catechizandis rudibus* (CSEL 46:121–78)
Ciu.	*De ciuitate Dei* (CCSL 47–48)
Conf.	*Confessionum libri XIII* (CCSL 27:1–273)
Cons.	*De consensu euangelistarum* (CSEL 43)
Cresc.	*Contra Cresconium Donatistam* (CSEL 52:325–582)
Doct. Chr.	*De doctrina christiana* (CCSL 32:1–167)
Enchir.	*Enchiridion de fide, spe et caritate* (CCSL 46:49–114)
Ep.	*Epistulae* (CSEL 34, 44, 57, 58; CCSL 31–31B)

Ep. Io.	*In epistulam Iohannis ad Parthos tractatus* (PL 35:1977–2062)	
Eu. Io.	*In euangelium Iohannis tractatus* (CCSL 36)	
Faust.	*Contra Faustum Manichaeus* (CSEL 25.1:251–797)	
Gal.	*Expositio in epistulam ad Galatas* (CSEL 84:55–141)	
Gen. litt.	*De Genesi ad litteram* (CSEL 28.1:3–435)	
Gen. Man.	*De Genesi contra Manichaeos* (CSEL 91:67–172)	
Parm.	*Contra epistulam Parmeniani* (CSEL 51:19–141)	
Pecc. merit.	*De peccatorum meritis* (CSEL 60:3–151)	
Petil.	*Contra litteras Petiliani* (CSEL 52:3–227)	
Psal.	*Enarrationes in Psalmos* (CCSL 38–40; CSEL 93.1A–95.5)	
Qu. eu.	*Quaestionum euangelicarum libri II* (CCSL 44B:1–118)	
Quaest.	*De diuersis quaestionibus* (CCSL 44A:11–249)	
Rom. prop.	*Expositio quarundam propositionum ex epistula apostoli ad Romanos* (CSEL 84:3–52)	
Serm.	*Sermones* (PL 38–39; CCSL 41, 41Aa, 41Ba)	
Serm. Dolb.	*Sermones a Dolbeau editi* (Dolbeau, Vingt-six Sermons)	
Serm. Guelf.	*Sermones Moriniani ex collectione Guelferbytana* (MA 1:450–585)	
Simpl.	*De diuersis quaestionibus ad Simplicianum* (CCSL 44:7–91)	
Trin.	*De Trinitate* (CCSL 50–50A)	

Cyprian

Demet.	*Ad Demetrianum* (CCSL 3A:35–51)
Dom. orat.	*De Dominica oratione* (CCSL 3A:90–113)
Eleem.	*De opere et eleemosynis* (CCSL 3A:55–72)
Ep.	*Epistulae* (CCSL 3A–B)
Hab. uirg.	*De habitu uirginum* (CSEL 3.1:187–205)
Laps.	*De lapsis* (CCSL 3:221–42)
Mort.	*De mortalitate* (CCSL 3A:17–32)
Sent.	*Sententiae episcoporum de haereticis baptizandis* (CCSL 3E)

Unit. eccl.	*De catholicae ecclesiae unitate* (CCSL 3:249–68)

Leo

Ep.	*Epistulae* (PL 54, 593–1218)
Serm.	*Sermones* xcvi (PL 54, 141–468)

Optatus of Milevis

Parm.	*Contra Parmenianum Donatistam* (CSEL 26:3–182)

Tertullian

An.	*De anima* (CCSL 2:781–869)
Apol.	*Apologeticus* (CCSL 1:85–171)
Bapt.	*De baptismo* (CCSL 1:277–95)
Carn. Chr.	*De carne Christi* (CCSL 2:873–917)
Cast.	*De exhortatione castitatis* (CCSL 2:1015–35)
Cor.	*De corona militis* (CCSL 2:1039–65)
Fug.	*De fuga in persecutione* (CCSL 2:1135–55)
Idol.	*De idolatria* (CCSL 2:1101–124)
Ieiun.	*De ieiunio aduersus Psychicos* (CCSL 2:1257–77)
Marc.	*Aduersus Marcionem* (CCSL 1:441–726)
Mart.	*Ad martyras* (CCSL 1:3–8)
Mon.	*De monogamia* (CCSL 2:1229–53)
Nat.	*Ad nationes* (CCSL 1:11–75)
Or.	*De oratione* (CCSL 1:257–74)
Paen.	*De paenitentia* (CCSL 1:321–40)
Pat.	*De patientia* (CCSL 1:299–317)
Praescr.	*De praescriptione haereticorum* (CCSL 1:187–224)
Prax.	*Aduersus Praxeam*
Pud.	*De pudicitia* (CCSL 2:1281–1330)
Res.	*De resurrectione mortuorum* (CCSL 1:921–1012)
Scap.	*Ad Scapulam* (CCSL 2:1127–32)
Scorp.	*Scorpiace* (CCSL 2:1069–97)
Spec.	*De spectaculis* (CCSL 1:227–53)
Ux.	*Ad uxorem* (CCSL 1:373–94)
Uirg.	*De uirginibus uelandis* (CCSL 2:1209–26)

Tyconius Afer

    Reg.   *Liber regularum* (Texts and Studies, 3.1, 1894; reprint, 2004)

Introduction

In the world of antiquity, religion was a communal and civic reality. To be a member of society meant to adhere to some form of religious devotion and identity. In the Roman Empire of the third century CE, the emperor was given god-like status and required veneration, often in the form of ritual sacrifices. Roman citizens were expected to participate in public and private ceremonies in order to offer worship to the pantheon of greater and lesser gods. Virtually all aspects of life were touched by religion.

As the city of Rome grew and the empire expanded, the Romans encountered people who worshiped strange gods and engaged in bizarre practices. By the first century CE, Jewish communities had sprung up in many cities of the empire. The Jews worshiped an invisible God, observed a Sabbath, abstained from pork, and most importantly, refused to participate in the worship of Roman gods and to offer sacrifices at their temples. Accommodations were made for Jewish communities by local magistrates, allowing them to gather on particular days and to follow their religious observances.[1]

Christianity posed a new challenge to the Roman empire. Whereas Jews were an ancient people from a particular land, Christians arose in the first century from groups of Jews and Gentiles who committed themselves to a new way of life. They rejected Roman religious rituals and would not participate in any practices tainted by what they deemed idolatry. This meant refusing to eat meat sacrificed to idols, avoiding public games, and following a strict moral code. Since they refused to partake in the cult of worship, Christians were called "superstitious" by some Romans and were considered a nuisance. Others considered them a seditious group and a threat to the empire. The Romans believed that religion sustained the life of the state and guaranteed its success. The new Christian movement undermined the flourishing of the empire.

The problem of Christianity was handled in different ways by imperial rulers. The earliest document about Christians by a Roman official was written by Pliny, governor of the province of Bithynia in Asia Minor, to the emperor Trajan. Pliny described Christians as a superstitious cult. The contemporary historian Tacitus had much stronger words. Christians were deadly, mischievous, impious, and hostile to humanity precisely because of their denial of Roman religion and society. Porphyry called Christians atheists who had apostasized from the customs of the ancestors.[2] They were a contamination that needed to be driven out of society in order to restore proper worship to the gods.

From the Christian perspective, the Romans were the ones guilty of idolatry, impurity, and false worship. Christians offered true worship to the one God. They declared Jesus of Nazareth the Son of God, Messiah, and Lord, and they believed that Jesus had risen from the dead. They eagerly awaited his return and believed that the end of time was imminent. Jesus would return to raise the dead, to offer final judgment, and to establish the kingdom of God in definitive fashion. As they awaited his second coming, they were obliged to follow his teaching, which meant following the ten commandments, loving God and neighbor, and offering prayers, fasting, and almsgiving. They collected sacred texts, known as the Scriptures, and gathered together regularly for worship. The earliest Christians became organized under the leadership of bishops who performed their religious rituals. They shared with the Jews a strong sense of community life through faith and practice that distinguished them from other groups in society.[3] Since they steadfastly rejected participation in the Roman cult, they were deemed dangerous and were increasingly scrutinized by imperial officials.

During the first century of Christianity in the empire, the persecution of Christians was sporadic. The first decrees were targeted against Christian leaders and property. In some places, Christians were not sought out, but if they were found and refused to sacrifice to the gods, they were subject to punishments, including torture and death. Despite persecution, Christian communities continued to grow in places such as Rome, Constantinople, Alexandria, Antioch, and North Africa. There were several sustained periods of persecution, but the first empire-wide persecution of Christians took place under the emperor Decius (249–251).

Under the constant threat of persecution, the earliest Christian communities were engaged in a dynamic process of self-understanding and self-preservation as the Christian church. The onset of persecution led Christians to consider the criteria for ecclesial membership. What did it mean to be a member of the church? What was the nature of the church, and what constituted the church's unity? What would happen to those who committed serious sins such as apostasy and idolatry? Would they be permitted to return?

Questions about identity arose among Christian communities throughout the empire, but the earliest extant sources in Latin that explored the nature of the church came from North Africa. Tertullian of Carthage is often considered the first theologian of Western Christianity. He lived and wrote in the context of a persecuted church that was seeking to define what it meant to be a faithful community of Christians. What was necessary for initiation into the church? What sins were grave enough to require expulsion from the community? Once expelled, was it possible to be readmitted? Was membership in the church necessary for the forgiveness of sins and eternal salvation? The answers to such questions depended upon the practices, Scriptural interpretation, and theological traditions of early Christians in the Roman world.

This study returns to the early centuries of Western Christianity in order to explore how the first Latin theologians forged a discernible doctrine of the nature, ends, and boundaries of the church. The following chapters analyze the trajectory of Latin ecclesiology among influential figures including Tertullian of Carthage, Cyprian of Carthage, Augustine of Hippo, and Pope Leo I. These church leaders left indelible contributions to the Christian tradition, and their works shed light on how early Christians in the Latin West understood the criteria for membership in the church. Each one of these great thinkers developed a distinctive ecclesiology, yet all of them attested to the four traditional marks of the church, albeit in different ways: the church is 1) one, 2) holy, 3) catholic, and 4) apostolic. In addition, ecclesiology was necessarily related to soteriology. As Cyprian famously declared, there is no salvation outside of the church (*salus extra ecclesiam non est*).[4] This claim holds true for these fathers of the church, but its meaning developed over the course of the first five centuries of Latin Christianity.

OVERVIEW OF CHAPTERS

In order to understand the meaning of the church, we must first grasp the history of the Christian communities in which the fathers lived, taught, and wrote. For each figure in the following chapters, we will consider his life, ecclesial and historical contexts, ritual practices (especially baptism, the Eucharist, and reconciliation), interpretation of the Scriptures, and theological development. Scholars have noted that in early Christianity, ecclesiology was not treated as an isolated subject for theological consideration. There were no treatises dedicated solely to the church in the East or West, perhaps with the exception of Cyprian's *On the Unity of the Church*.[5] Ecclesiology developed in relation to other fundamental theological topics, such as Christology and pneumatology, and in the midst of disputes over practice, doctrine, and jurisdiction. The early theologians reflected on the church in their writings and in their preaching, and an examination of their views must account for their most important ecclesiological works in their proper contexts. This study brings together the historical and literary evidence for Christian practice and theology in order to show how Christian practice and doctrine interacted in the formation of early Latin ecclesiology.

Chapter 1 examines the life and thought of Tertullian of Carthage (c. 160–225), whose writings touched on nearly every aspect of Christian life and supplied much of the theological vocabulary of Western Christianity.[6] Although he received a first-rate Roman education in rhetoric, Tertullian lived in North Africa, where Christians bore multiple identities as Romans and Africans.[7] There he came into contact with a number of indigenous religions and pagan cults. The first evidence of Christianity in North Africa was the condemnation and martyrdom of twelve Christian converts near the end of the second century. Tertullian lived during a time of sporadic persecution. To be Christian in his context meant to reject traditional practices of Punic and Roman idolatry, and to commit oneself to Christ by faithful observance of the church's ritual, moral, and ascetic practices.[8] Initiation into the Christian community normally took place through a period of preparation known as the catechumenate before reception into the Christian mysteries by the ritual washing of baptism. Baptized Christians were cleansed from their sins and received the gift of the Holy Spirit. Only after baptism were Christians permitted to partake of eucharistic communion, which was the central liturgical worship of the Christian church.

Christians were required to forsake all forms of idolatry, and they could not come into contact with any of the idolatrous practices or objects used in pagan ceremonies. Idolatry was spread like a contagious disease by means of contact with material objects. Tertullian and his fellow Christians believed that they could be contaminated by evil spirits, for the demons could inhabit idols and places such as pagan shrines and public shows.[9] Therefore, all Christians were forbidden from partaking in any civic ceremonies or celebrations that could lead to contamination. The church had to remain free from the stain of idolatry. Anyone who committed grave sins such as idolatry, apostasy, or murder could not be admitted to eucharistic fellowship. In Tertullian's view, those who committed serious sins were permanently excluded from the church, for the church could not tolerate their presence among the faithful. As the body of Christ and the temple of the Holy Spirit, the church had to remain pure by expelling the impure. There could be no taint of sin in the church because the church was the dwelling place of God.

Tertullian maintained a clear doctrine of the apostolicity of the church. The church's bishops were successors of the apostles, and this apostolic succession preserved the true doctrine given to the apostles from Christ. Recognition of this apostolicity was necessary in order to remain in the unity of the church, and heretics forfeited this unity by their erroneous teaching and their separation from communities founded by the apostles. While Tertullian posited this strong view of the apostolic unity of the church, he also criticized members of the hierarchy, especially those bishops who attempted to forgive grave sins and to readmit sinners to eucharistic communion. According to Tertullian, this violated the virginal purity of the church, encouraged further sin, and was an overreach of episcopal authority. Tertullian argued that only God could forgive certain sins, and even as successors of the apostles, the bishops could not forgive that which only God could.

In addition, Tertullian began to privilege those spiritual members who demonstrated the presence and activity of the Holy Spirit by visions, prophecy, and miraculous healings. For Tertullian, the Holy Spirit belonged to the whole church, not merely the clergy, for all of the members formed the one body of Christ. The reception of holy orders did not guarantee the work of the Spirit, for even clergy could commit serious sins. In Tertullian's later works, under greater influence from Montanism, there was an increasing tension between the invisible communion of charity and the visible, institutional church as represented by the clergy. The church's invisible union in charity had primacy over visible apostolic unity. In Tertullian's view, there was no salvation outside of the charity given by the Holy Spirit. This charity was normally administered by means of the sacraments, especially baptism, but it could be lost by grave sin, and sinners had to be expelled from the church's perfect spiritual communion. Thus, Tertullian held a perfectionist and exclusionist ecclesiology, wherein the church's purity and holiness depended upon preservation from the pollution of sin.[10] Tertullian's ecclesiology can also be described as rigorist, for the church's purity was maintained by a rigorism that refused to reconcile those guilty of serious sins since, in Tertullian's mind, the church did not have the power to forgive grave sins.

Chapter 2 discusses Cyprian (c. 200–258), who became bishop of Carthage during periods of sustained persecution. Cyprian and his episcopal colleagues had to deal with the difficult issue of readmitting to communion those who had committed apostasy and idolatry in varying degrees. Under what conditions, if any, could the lapsed return to the fellowship of the church and participate in eucharistic communion? Cyprian followed Tertullian and the North African tradition's understanding of the contagion of sin. Initially, Cyprian and some clergy decided to exclude from communion those who had sacrificed, as well as those who had cheated by obtaining a certificate of sacrifice (*libellus*) by other means.[11] Genuine penitents could only be restored on their deathbed. However, Cyprian changed his mind after listening to his fellow North African bishops who had gathered in formal councils. After some deliberation, Cyprian determined that those guilty of serious sins such as idolatry and apostasy could be readmitted to eucharistic fellowship after participating in a process of penance and reconciliation, a process that was overseen by the local bishop. In some instances, this meant public confession of sin, public forms of penance such as the wearing of sackcloth and ashes, and penitential practices including prayer, fasting, and almsgiving. After sufficient completion of this process, the penitents would receive the laying on of hands from the bishop in order receive the Holy Spirit and the gift of charity. They were then permitted to be readmitted to the eucharistic fellowship of the church.

Cyprian provided a more moderate approach than the rigorist tradition represented by Tertullian. In order to support this change in practice, Cyprian developed an ecclesiology in which the bishops, as successors of the apostles, received the power to forgive the sins of any because of the sending of the Holy Spirit from Christ in John 20:22–23. God could forgive even grave sins through the mediation of the bishops. The distinctive feature of Cyprian's theology is that the bishop maintained the unity and charity of the church precisely by remaining in communion with the episcopal college of bishops throughout the world. The apostle Peter, as head of the apostles, represented this union of the apostolic college, and the successors of the apostles must remain in this unity in order to receive the Holy Spirit and to exercise their ministry. If a bishop cut himself off from this unity, he no longer had the power to sanctify, and he could not effectively preside over the sacraments. Since he did not have the Spirit, he could not sanctify the baptismal waters or offer the Eucharist. A schismatic bishop did not have valid sacraments. This led to a controversy with Stephen, the bishop of Rome, who argued that schismatics did indeed have valid sacraments, specifically valid baptism. This conflict was never fully resolved because both Cyprian and Stephen were martyred under the persecution of Valerian. In his innovative ecclesiology, Cyprian privileged the bishops in terms of the church's unity. In order to preserve unity with the church, the bishop must remain in the unity of the episcopal college. Otherwise, he and his congregation were cut off from the church's unity in charity and in the Spirit.

Chapter 3 explores the ecclesiology of Augustine of Hippo (c. 354–430), one of the most influential theologians in the history of Christianity. Augustine lived during a time of transition in the relationship between Christianity and the Roman empire after the imperial decree of religious freedom in 313 known as the Edict of Milan. By the second half of the fourth century, Christianity had become the dominant religion of the empire. Like the earlier generations of Christians, Augustine sought ways to distinguish the church from other groups, but without the constant threat of persecution. Although he did not face violent persecution, Augustine did have to grapple with political instability in the empire, culminating with the fall of Rome to Alaric and the Goths in 410 and the barbarian invasion of North Africa. Later in his life as a pastor and bishop, he had to make a defense for Christian thought and practice after many blamed the Christian religion for loss of imperial power due to the suppression of the Roman pantheon. This was the task he took up in his monumental work, *City of God*, which brought together many strands of his thought on the church. His ideas on the church developed in the midst of multiple controversies with Christian groups, including the Manicheans, Donatists, and Pelagians. His ecclesiology was also on display in his preaching, as occasioned by the church's contact with communities such as the Donatists.

Against the Donatists, Augustine attempted to mitigate the rigorism of Tertullian while maintaining Cyprian's insistence upon unity around the episcopacy. Augustine claimed the authority of Cyprian, which the Donatists also claimed, even though Augustine offered a different picture of the church's unity in charity and in the Spirit than Cyprian. Relying on the arguments of the North African bishop Optatus of Milevis, Augustine insisted that the holiness of the minister did not determine the efficacy of the sacrament. Instead, it was Christ who worked through the minister in order to effect the sacrament. Contrary to the Donatist position, the moral condition of the minister did not determine the validity of the sacrament, although any who participated unworthily in the sacraments did so at their own peril. Contrary to Cyprian's position, Augustine argued that the bishop's unity or disunity with the episcopal college did not determine the presence and activity of the Holy Spirit in the administration of the sacraments. The same principle used against the Donatists applied, namely, that Christ worked in and through the sacraments. The church's charity did not belong to the bishops alone, for the charity poured out upon our hearts by the Spirit (Rom. 5:5) was a gift that belonged to the entire body of Christ, head and members. When a validly ordained minister celebrated the sacraments, Christ and the Spirit were at work to unite the one body in charity. Those who were in schism, however, immediately cut themselves off from these effects.

By emphasizing the church's unity in charity among the entire body, clergy and laity alike, Augustine accepted and modified Tertullian's understanding of the charity given to the whole church by the Spirit. Unlike Tertullian, Augustine followed Cyprian in finding ways to reconcile sinners to the church. Augustine affirmed the need for apostolic succession in order for the bishop to possess the proper authority to determine the penitential program for reconciliation. Yet Augustine offered a unique position by declaring that the whole Christ united in charity offered the forgiveness of sins to the penitents. The church was constituted by the communion of the head and members united in the invisible bond of charity, which included the saints in heaven and the holy ones on earth, and this communion forgave the sins of those who repented. This did not denigrate the power of Christ in any way, for such forgiveness was only made possible by the sacrifice of the head, nor did it eliminate the role of the clergy, who administered the sacrament of reconciliation. However, Augustine included the members of Christ's body as part of the intercession on behalf of penitents in order to receive forgiveness. It was essential to remain in union with the bishop, but the bishop did not determine the efficacy of the Spirit. The unity of the whole Christ, head and members, forgave serious sins and readmitted penitents into the church's communion by means of the penitential program determined by the bishop.

Augustine's ecclesiology was marked by subtlety, complexity, and necessary distinctions without separation. The church was an invisible communion of charity and a visible community of clergy and laity celebrating the sacraments. The invisible and visible could be distinguished but not separated. Only the members united in charity constituted the one body of Christ, but entrance into the one body was mediated by the sacraments of the visible, Catholic Church. Building upon the thought of the dissident Donatist theologian Tyconius, Augustine held that the visible church contained both the good and the wicked, grain and chaff, elect and reprobate. There were two cities, heavenly and earthly, with two kinds of citizens. During this time, the citizens of the cities were mixed together, but at the end time, they will be separated definitively. In the meantime, the city of God includes the members in heaven and the holy ones on pilgrimage on earth. The whole city was united as one fellowship and one sacrifice at the daily eucharistic offering of the visible church. The holy ones on pilgrimage were joined in charity to the fellowship enjoyed by the angels and saints in heaven. This was the unity in charity symbolized and made efficacious in the celebration of the Eucharist.

In the visible church, the good and the wicked were intermingled, but this did not make the church impure. Augustine argued that the charity of the saints given by the Holy Spirit could tolerate any scandal or sin. While it was necessary for sinners to be reconciled prior to participation in eucharistic communion, those who ate or drank unworthily did so at their own destruction. They could not be joined to the church's unity in charity, but they also did not harm the communion of the saints, for the power of the Spirit was not diminished by the presence of sinners.

In addition, Augustine maintained that while incorporation into the church's unity in charity normally occurred by means of baptism, it was possible for some to be joined to charity of the church without having received the ritual cleansing. For instance, those catechumens who were martyred experienced baptism by blood, an ancient tradition affirmed by both Tertullian and Cyprian. Augustine went further by asserting that those who sought the spiritual things of God but died before receiving the sacrament could be united to the charity of the church at some future time. Indeed, Augustine declared that there are some outside of the church who will be in, and some inside who will be out. In Augustine's theology, this did not obviate the visible church's ritual of baptism, rather, it attested to the power of the Spirit to work beyond visible limits. God worked through the visible sacraments but was not limited by them. Nevertheless, the Spirit always brought those who were outside into the same unity of charity mediated by the sacraments of the Catholic Church. There were not two separate communions, one visible and one invisible. There was only one communion constituted by the invisible bond of charity. Those who participated unworthily in the sacraments cut themselves off from this unity. Therefore, according to Augustine's theology of the church, there was only one, holy, Catholic, and apostolic church, outside of which there was no salvation, even if some of the members were outside of the church's visible unity. Salvation could only come from participation in charity by the gift of the Holy Spirit, and the Spirit brought all of the members to share in the one communion of the church. According to Augustine, there is no salvation outside of charity.

In Chapter 4, we turn to Pope Leo I (c. 400–461), also remembered as Leo the Great. Like Augustine before him, Leo lived during a time when Christianity had expanded to become the dominant religion of the empire. Leo's ecclesiology built upon the tradition he had received while further delineating the unique authority of the bishop of Rome as the successor of Peter. Leo became bishop of Rome during a time of external and internal conflict. The city of Rome had fallen siege to the Goths, Vandals, and barbarian invaders. The empire was weakened under poor leadership and political turmoil. In the church, the Christological debates among Christians, particularly in the East, continued with renewed vigor and demanded resolution. Leo attempted to intervene, sometimes unsuccessfully, in order to exercise his role as head of the church.

Leo constructed his understanding of papal authority based upon the primacy given to Peter by Christ in Matthew 16. As the rock upon which the church was built, Peter shared in the mission of Christ, the true head, rock, and foundation of the church. The graces from Christ the head were mediated to the church by means of Peter, who was given partnership in the building up of the temple of God. According to God's plan, Christ chose Peter as the head of the apostles to govern the church, preserve the truth, and mediate grace to the whole world. As the successor of Peter, the bishop of Rome received the authority to govern over ecclesiastical matters, settle doctrinal disputes, and bring the Gospel to all nations.

Leo worked tirelessly to strengthen the church in Rome and to establish the pope's role as a leader in civic affairs. In his letters to political authorities, Leo emphasized God's plan for the emperor to provide protection and care for the church. God had chosen the city of Rome, once the eternal city, to be the hill upon which the city of God would be set in order to be a light to the nations. The emperor was given power by God to protect the church, which might include deposing heretics. At the same time, the emperor had to respect the authority of the bishop of Rome, who was the head of the church and who determined what constituted heresy. Leo took upon himself the responsibility to serve as the spiritual head of the entire world. While he maintained the Augustinian distinction between the two cities, defined by the love of God and the love of the world, Leo believed that the church had to be engaged in society in order to restore order and to spread the Gospel. Theologically, the church and the world remained separate. In this historical setting, the church had to become an active player in society.

In Leo's thought, the pope's leadership was exercised by preserving true doctrine, exerting jurisdictional authority, and expanding the church's reach to the ends of the earth. The church's unity in charity flowed from the graces that were mediated from Christ the head to his body the church by means of the successor of Peter. Thus, unity in the church meant unity with the Roman bishop. Leo's ecclesiology was missional in its ends and papal in its means. Salvation was found in the unity of the Catholic Church, with the pope as the visible head of the church and the spiritual head of the world.

The doctrine of the church in early Latin Christianity took shape in the midst of external and internal conflicts. The interplay between history, practice, and theology was evident in the formation of Latin ecclesiology. Each one of the Latin fathers offered a unique contribution to the teaching on the church, yet each one affirmed that the church was one and holy, visible and invisible, Catholic and apostolic. The church was a visible community bound by the invisible bond of charity. Participation in the rituals of the visible church was a necessary but not sufficient condition for salvation. To be a member of the church meant to be joined to the church's unity in charity. The sacraments of the church mediated charity and incorporated new members into the one body of Christ, particularly baptism. The new members of the Christian church had to reject their former worldliness while swearing allegiance to Christ. They remained distinct from the world in which they lived, and they were permitted varying levels of participation in society, depending upon how such participation touched on their spiritual commitments. Christians were in the world, but not of it. They were members of a community defined by charity, the love of God and neighbor, which was mediated invisibly by the sacraments and enacted by practices such as prayer, fasting, and almsgiving. This was the way of salvation, for in early Christianity, salvation meant participation in charity as a gift given by God and shared among the body of Christ. There was no salvation outside of the one church founded by Christ and empowered by the Spirit. However, the Spirit could work invisibly in order to bring new members into the one Christ, head and members. Thus, the church was a mystery with visible and invisible dimensions that were distinct but inseparable. This doctrine has remained a distinguishing feature of Western Christianity from the early church to the present.

NOTES

1. Robert Louis Wilken, *Liberty in the Things of God: The Christian Origins of Religious Freedom* (New Haven: Yale University Press, 2019), 9.

2. Wilken, *Liberty in the Things of God*, 19; Robert Lewis Wilken, *The Christians as the Romans Saw Them* (New Haven: Yale University Press, 1984), 126–63.

3. Everett Ferguson, "Community and Worship," in *The Routledge Companion to Early Christian Thought*, ed. D. Jeffrey Bingham (New York: Routledge, 2010), 313–30.

4. Cyprian, *Ep.* 73.21.2; CCSL 3C.555.

5. "The first believers did not write treatises on the church in the way they wrote them on Christ or the Holy Spirit or other topics. In the vast range of early Christian literature one will find only one treatise, Cyprian's *On the Unity of the Church*, devoted more or less directly to an understanding of the church, but even there the issue is *unity* rather than church"; E. Glenn Hinson, *Understandings of the Church*, in *Sources of Early Christian Thought*, ed. William G. Rusch (Philadelphia: Fortress Press, 1986), 1; G. R. Evans, "The Church in the Early Christian Centuries: Ecclesiological Consolidation," in *The Routledge Companion to the Christian Church*, eds. Gerard Mannion and Lewis S. Mudge (New York: Routledge, 2007), 28; Henry Chadwick, *The Church in Ancient Society: From Galilee to Gregory the Great* (New York: Oxford University Press, 2001), 154; David Rankin, *Tertullian and the Church* (Cambridge: Cambridge University Press, 1995), 1; Avery Dulles and Patrick Granfield, *The Church: A Bibliography* (Wilmington: Michael Glazier, 1985), 9–12; Robert Eno, *Teaching Authority in the Early Church* (Wilmington: Michael Glazier, 1984), 13–29. According to Robert Evans, "Latin theology none the less shows a tendency to be concerned . . . with the form and character of Christian society, or, to speak more briefly, with the doctrine of the Church"; *One and Holy: The Church in Latin Patristic Thought* (London: S.P.C.K., 1972), 1.

6. Geoffrey D. Dunn, *Tertullian* (New York: Routledge, 2004), 10–11.

7. On this point, see David Wilhite, *Ancient African Christianity: An Introduction to a Unique Context and Tradition* (New York: Routledge, 2017), 14–15; Éric Rebillard, *Christians and Their Many Identities in Late Antiquity, North Africa, 200–450 CE* (Ithaca: Cornell University Press, 2012).

8. J. Patout Burns, Robin M. Jensen, et al., *Christianity in Roman Africa: The Development of Its Practices and Beliefs* (Grand Rapids: Eerdmans, 2014), 601.

9. Wilhite, *Ancient African Christianity*, 121.

10. Rankin, *Tertullian and the Church*, 92–98.

11. Stuart G. Hall, "The Early Idea of the Church," in *The First Christian Theologians: An Introduction to Theology in the Early Church*, ed. G. R. Evans (Malden: Blackwell, 2004), 52.

Chapter One

Tertullian of Carthage

Tertullian of Carthage was the first Christian theologian to write in Latin whose works are extant. Tertullian's teachings have had a profound impact upon Christianity in the Latin West. While he is often considered the first of the Western fathers, Tertullian lived and wrote in North Africa. His ecclesiology developed in the context of the sporadic persecution of the church. For Tertullian, to be a member of the church meant to be set apart from the world, for Christians "should be in the world (*saeculo*), but not of it."[1] This distinction between the church and the world persisted over the course of Tertullian's life, as evident in his later so-called Montanist writings. Scholars today generally reject the idea that Tertullian left the Catholic Church to become a Montanist.[2] Whether or not there was a discernible turn toward Montanism later in Tertullian's life, it was clear that in Tertullian's view, the church was the one medium of holiness and salvation. Membership in the church and participation in the sacred mysteries required holiness of life by ascetic practice, the rejection of serious sins such as idolatry and apostasy, and ethical conduct.

This chapter analyzes Tertullian's ecclesiology as it developed in the context of North African Christianity, with attention to the historical context, practice, liturgical worship, and theology of the church. Tertullian's thought demonstrates the impact of North African practice upon early Christian doctrine. His distinctive view of the church was also based upon his interpretation of Scriptural texts. Tertullian used Biblical images in order to illustrate how the church was one and holy. The members of the church had to remain pure in order to participate in the sacraments. Ultimately, the church was constituted by the spiritual ones, who manifested charismatic gifts and were free from serious sin. As a leading theologian in North Africa, Tertullian was one of the most significant and controversial figures of early Latin Christianity.

TERTULLIAN'S LIFE

Tertullian's life has been made accessible due to modern scholarship, but the details of his life remain obscure.[3] Tertullian reportedly belonged to a family of status and received an excellent education in Greco-Roman sources, progressing from grammar to rhetoric.[4] Likely born around 160, Tertullian's first writings appear in the 190s. Recent research has shown that although Tertullian used legal metaphors, his works do not demonstrate expertise in jurisprudence, and thus there is no basis for the claim that Tertullian was a Roman jurist.[5] He is best understood as a classically trained rhetorician, like many of the early church fathers in the West and East. Tertullian was raised a pagan and converted to Christianity in response to some event that led him to reject his former way of life.[6] Although Jerome claimed Tertullian became a priest, Tertullian himself seemed to deny any such ordination.[7] Some have speculated that Tertullian was a lay elder as head of a house church in North Africa.[8] Most likely, Tertullian was married, and in his writings, he advocated that a Christian should not seek remarriage after the death of one's spouse.[9]

Although Tertullian has been interpreted primarily as a Roman, there is no evidence that he ever went to Rome.[10] Tertullian lived his entire life in Carthage, which by the end of the second century had a population of around 700,000.[11] The Romans ruled North Africa from the end of the final Punic war (146 BCE) until the fifth century CE. In 42 CE, the entire region became a senatorial province ruled by a proconsul, and North Africa consisted of several provinces until the late third century. Romanization occurred gradually as coastal cities that allied with Rome during the Punic Wars received full citizenship and favorable trading rights, while some Punic towns were granted lesser status as *coloniae* or *municipia*.[12] In general, urban areas welcomed Roman customs and adopted Latin as their language, while many rural sites retained Punic traditions and language. Archaeology has revealed traces of ancient urban habitations, such as Punic trading posts, that developed into important cities. African urbanization was a key factor in Romanization and the growth of Christianity.[13] However, as recent scholars have argued, Romanization or colonization did not mean that the empire imposed its will upon passive subjects.[14] Local indigenous groups retained their own agency and customs. Scholars now understand that Africa retained its pre-Roman heritage throughout the Roman period, as African languages (such as Libyan and Punic), art, religions, and practices survived.[15]

Tertullian retained his African identity while living during a time of Roman political colonization and religious persecution.[16] The earliest reference to Tertullian is to *Tertullianus Afer*, Tertullian the African.[17] When Tertullian wrote his full name as *Septimus Tertullianus*, it was shared with the emperor of Rome, Septimius Severus, who was from Leptis Magna in modern Libya and became the first emperor from North Africa. As scholars have noted, Tertullian and other early Christians inhabited multiple identities, and in Tertullian's case, this meant claiming African and Roman lineage.[18]

THE CHURCH IN NORTH AFRICA

The origins of Christianity in Africa remain uncertain.[19] The first evidence for Christianity in North Africa appeared with the account of *The Acts of the Scillitans*, which survives in several Latin manuscripts as well as a Greek version.[20] In the year 180 CE, a group of twelve Christians from the region of Scilli, about 150 km west of Carthage, were brought before the governor's tribunal in Carthage.[21] They were put to death by the Roman proconsul for proclaiming Jesus as *Dominus*, or Lord.[22] This process put into practice Trajan's rescript of 112, which set a precedent for formally charging Christians with apostasy. Strikingly, the names of the twelve martyrs were typical African names. While this was the first surviving account of Christian presence in North Africa, Christianity was known publicly in the African provinces before 180. The catacombs of Hadrumetum contained inscriptions of symbols such as the good shepherd, the dove, and the fish that were characteristically Christian.[23] Burial sites were important for North African Christianity, as apparent in the burial shrines of the martyrs, where rituals were performed and buildings were erected for Christian worship.[24] Prior to Christian burials in the Hadrumetum catacombs, there is evidence of a local church in the early second century.[25] However, the earliest Christian records in North Africa are *The Acts of the Scillitans* and *The Passion of Perpetua and Felicity*. Tertullian was familiar with these accounts, and the stories of the martyrs played an important role in the formation of early North African Christian identity.

Perpetua and her companions were martyred on March 7, 203, likely in the arena of Carthage. In the written record, there is an emphasis upon prophecies, visions, and the Spirit. This has raised the question of the influence of Montanism, which began around 165–170 in Asia Minor with the prophets Montanus, Priscilla, and Maximilla. However, scholars have generally rejected the label of Montanism for *The Passion of Perpetua and Felicity* as the alleged Montanism found in North Africa differed from the New Prophecy that emerged in Phrygia.[26] While this text is not properly called Montanist, it is clear that visions and prophecies were common features of

Christianity in early North Africa. Other significant features of Perpetua's church in Carthage at this time include a clearly developed clergy (bishop, priest, deacon) and Christian rituals, such as baptism, the passing of the kiss, the agape meal, and perhaps other elements of liturgical worship. These rituals were essential identity markers for Christians in North Africa. While there is no doubt that local indigenous religions influenced expressions of Christianity, there were defining features of Christianity that distinguished Christian communities from local religions, such as the celebration of the sacraments of baptism and the Eucharist.

The description of the Christian community found in *The Passion of Perpetua and Felicity* concurred with Tertullian's writings. The earliest Christian texts from North Africa indicate that multiple social identities were in play. Christians lived in a society shaped not only by Greco-Roman influences but also by the Punic heritage, particularly in Carthage. One crucial aspect of the Punic tradition in North Africa was the presence of Punic cults and the devotion associated with such indigenous religions.[27] The traditional practices of self-sacrifice connected with the cults of Baal/Saturn and Tanit/Juno/Caelestis might have influenced African Christians in terms of their willingness to die as martyrs for Christ.[28] Roman North Africa had an array of cults, including temples to Jupiter, Juno, Minerva, Saturn, Apollo, Cybele, Ceres, and Asclepius, among others.[29] Berber and Punic elements became mixed with Greco-Roman practices creating a hybrid of cults. In this religious context, it is significant that Christians who refused to worship Roman deities and to make sacrifices to Roman officials were, at times, spoken of as being made into Punic priests and priestesses.[30] New Christians in North Africa did not understand themselves simply as anti-Roman. Rather, it is important to remember that these Christians were African but they rejected the Romano-African sacrifices and rituals demanded by governing officials that were contrary to the Gospel. Thus, Christians gained a distinctive identity by their worship. At the same time, the Roman and African identities of Christians certainly influenced their Christianity. Christians in North Africa were willing to sacrifice themselves as martyrs in contradistinction to the sacrifices of indigenous religions.

Another key feature of the social and religious context of North African Christianity was the role of local African elites. Many of the elites embodied at least two distinct social identities: 1) African, meaning they were descended from Libyan, Punic, Mauretanian, or other groups; 2) Roman, meaning they embraced *Romanitas* by speaking Latin, wearing togas instead of the African mantle or pallium, and seeking to rise in social rankings.[31] These elites attempted to mediate religion between Roman colonizers and indigenous people in order to establish special status. For instance, one expectation of elites was to sponsor public displays of loyalty by hosting games, festivals, and by constructing public buildings and monuments. During such displays, the gods would be invoked and sacrifices offered, thereby appeasing Roman leaders while also patronizing the local people. This system enabled the elites to play an important mediatory role between Roman rulers and the African people. Some scholars have argued that this might have contributed to the rise of persecution against Christians, for any disturbance of the practice of Romano-African sacrifices and rituals would have threatened the position of the elites.[32] Thus, they might have been motivated to bring accusations of Christian disturbances before the Roman officials, who did not seek out Christians following Trajan's directive. One African elite, Septimius Severus, became the first African emperor. His relationship to the elites, who viewed Christianity as a subversive religion that threatened their socio-political status, was essential to the persecution he enacted against Christians during his reign.

THE CHURCH IN CARTHAGE

Carthage was a large seaport and a prosperous city in the second century CE. The African church in Carthage, while aware of the Roman church and its policies, was largely independent and was led by a bishop, like most of the Christian communities in Africa.[33] According to some estimates, in the year 200, only about 0.35 percent of the population of Carthage was Christian.[34] Tertullian belonged to an elite group in terms of his literacy and education, for he acknowledged that most Christians were uneducated.[35] In his works, Tertullian claimed that the spread of Christianity across Africa was vast and amounted to almost a majority in every city, including Thysdrus and Hadrumetum and Uthina,[36] but such a claim was surely exaggerated. Nevertheless, by the middle of the third century, there was a Christian presence in over a hundred African cities, with communities in Mauretania, Tripolitana, and in the populous centers of Numidia.[37]

The Christian community in Carthage contained a broad cross-section of practice, as evident in Tertullian's writings. For Tertullian, as a representative of North African Christians in Carthage, the church and the world (*saeculum*) had to be distinct in order to preserve the church's holiness and purity.[38] Christians must not partake in non-Christian rituals and sacrifices, which amounted to idolatry and demon worship.[39] Even attendance at the circus or the theater could lead to contamination by evil spirits.[40] Wood and stone could be inhabited by demons who worked through them, and so Christians had to reject idolatrous things. Scholars have argued persuasively that Tertullian held a participatory ontology in which the spiritual pervades the material and the material can participate in the spiritual, thus avoiding a Gnostic form of Christianity that would deny such participation.[41] The material and the spiritual were distinct but inseparable, and Christians had to be vigilant against temptations to sin. Among other Christian practices and disciplines, Tertullian advocated modest dress, self-renunciation, fasting, and abstinence from sexual lust in order to avoid sin and to ward off evil spirits.[42] Tertullian's participatory ontology was operative in his understanding of baptism, whereby one's sins were washed away and the Holy Spirit was received.[43]

Baptism was an essential practice in the North African church that established a firm boundary between the church and the world. The baptismal oath was a repudiation of idolatry and a commitment to Christ, thus separating the Christian cult from those who continued to practice Greco-Roman and African polytheism.[44] According to Tertullian, baptism was necessary for salvation, and the church's baptism was the only one that counted, for heretical baptism was no baptism at all.[45] In Tertullian's setting in North Africa, it was common for parents to withhold baptism from children before they could make a sufficient profession of faith and a vow to live without committing serious sins. In Tertullian's view, infants had no sins to be forgiven.[46] However, some Christians were more anxious to secure baptism for their children, so infant baptism was practiced in some communities.

Tertullian held that baptism should be reserved for adults after an extended period of preparation, known as the catechumenate, which was necessary not only for doctrinal instruction but also for moral and spiritual transformation.[47] The candidates had to be well established in a life that rejected the idolatry of the surrounding culture. The preparation for baptism included practices such as prayer, fasting, acknowledging one's sins, and making an oath to God and the church. Tertullian's description of the ritual of baptism does not mention a pre-baptismal exorcism, although Tertullian was concerned with demonic presences.[48]

The water used in the ritual had to be sanctified by the power of the Holy Spirit.[49] The one being baptized was first cleansed from sins by the washing and then would receive the Holy Spirit by the imposition of hands.[50] The form of baptism in Tertullian's context was a triple immersion, in which faith in the Trinity and the church was confessed.[51] The washing with water was followed by anointing with oil and the imposition of hands to invite the Holy Spirit to bestow peace. Although the clergy were the typical celebrants of baptism, Tertullian held that any baptized person could confer baptism when necessary.[52] Tertullian affirmed that baptism was not repeatable, however, this did not mean that the heretics conferred baptism. Since they declared a different God and Christ, they could not receive or give the same baptism.[53] Tertullian recognized martyrdom as a baptism by blood that could substitute for the washing of water, as in the case of a catechumen who died before being baptized. Martyrdom could also restore baptism for those who had committed grave sin, according to God's just judgment.[54]

Christians participated in the eucharistic celebration only after receiving baptism. In Tertullian's time, there were different meal celebrations that could take place either in the evening or in the morning modeled after Christ's last supper with his disciples before his death. Over against the Romano-African sacrifices of the state cult, Christians emphasized the sacrificial character of the eucharistic ritual.[55] In his *Apology*, Tertullian outlined the order of the eucharistic service which included prayers, readings of sacred texts, and exhortations based on the Scriptures. He also described an evening meal in which the participants were drawn from all social classes, with an unusual respect shown for the poor.[56] In his treatise *On Prayer*, Tertullian described a morning sacrificial service with the reception of the Lord's body.[57] Tertullian understood the community's prayer as the sacrifice of Christians offered to the true God in place of the sacrifices offered by pagans to false gods.[58] Part of this offering was the sharing of the Eucharist, whereby Christians shared in the body and blood of Christ.[59]

In his eucharistic theology, Tertullian argued against those anti-materialists who rejected Christ's assumption of human flesh. Just as Christ used bread and wine at the last supper to institute the Eucharist, so Christ truly assumed a material body in the incarnation.[60] This argument was based upon church practice, for the church's liturgical worship demonstrated the significance of the material world and its relation to spiritual realities for Christians. Any contact with idolatrous sacrifices or rituals made Christians unfit for participation in eucharistic sacrifice.[61] Tertullian gave evidence for the practice of temporary excommunication for gulty sinners, followed by repentance and reinstatement.[62] He also indicated that certain sins, namely idolatry, adultery, and murder, resulted in permanent exclusion from communion.[63] We will return to the theological significance of the sacraments of baptism and the Eucharist for Tertullian's ecclesiology.

Tertullian's writings also offer evidence of the significance of martyrdom in early North African Christianity. Christians were called to give their lives in the battle against the enemy, that is, the devil and the demons who had dominion over the world.[64] Tertullian exhorted Christians to suffer in order to partake in the fullness of God's grace.[65] The tradition of North Africa was rightly called "the church of the martyrs." Christians were prepared to be participants in the spectacles of the world not by sacrificing to idols, but by becoming sacrifices to the true God.[66] Martyrdom was held up as the most blessed state, and those catechumens who were martyred were baptized in blood. Tertullian himself seems to have been converted by seeing the heroism and faith of the martyrs.

The persecution of Christians in North Africa occurred sporadically and locally, ignited usually by a pagan mob or by merchants whose products Christians were boycotting. Roman officials were reluctant to convict Christians, as Tertullian's works show.[67] As discussed earlier, the persecution of

Christians in North Africa could have been instigated by the elites in order to enhance their social status. In 197, Carthage endured persecution under Septimius Severus, the first emperor from Africa. Tertullian's *To the Martyrs* described how Christians were to respond. If brought to trial, Christians did not need to fear what to say, for the Holy Spirit would guide them (Matt. 10:19–20). The Holy Spirit resided in the imprisoned (confessors) and in those about to be martyred, and they had the power to absolve sins without the mediation of the clergy.[68] The end time was approaching, and martyrdom expedited the process (Rev. 6:9–11). Paradise awaited those who died for the faith,[69] and the true home of Christians was the heavenly Jerusalem. The church on earth must be willing to suffer and die in the midst of persecution.

From Tertullian's *To Scapula,* we know that the proconsul of Africa launched a fierce persecution of Christians in Mauretania and Numidia in 212. The onset of persecution led Christians to question if someone who had committed apostasy or other grave sins could be reconciled to the church. Could readmission be allowed, and if so, under what conditions? What kinds of penance were required, and who was empowered to grant forgiveness on behalf of God? Tertullian set penance within the general context of the forgiveness of sins in baptism. His works show that a ritual of repentance was practiced in the third century that included the public confession of sins, suspension from participation in the community's prayers and Eucharist, and the reception of penitential practices, some of which were private and some public.[70] Fasting was encouraged, along with prayers while kneeling and weeping.[71] Some wore sackcloth and ashes and gave up bathing; some begged the members of the community for intercessory prayers.[72] They also knocked on the door of the church, asking to be allowed back into the community.[73] The length of time for such public penances was not specified in Tertullian's writings, but apparently it was common for some penances to last as long as several years, depending upon the seriousness of the sin. Typically, the bishop determined the penitential program. When the process was sufficiently completed, they brought penitents into the church, and the bishop spoke a declarative absolution that forgave sins and loosened the bonds of the penitent.[74] This ritual would have been performed at an assembly of the whole community, which gathered for a morning prayer service.[75]

In his early treatise *On Penance* (c. 198), Tertullian warned that penance should be undertaken only once before baptism and once after. If a Christian returned to sin after baptism, there was a second opportunity for full and effective repentance, which could only be done once and thus was final.[76] In his later treatise *On Modesty* (c. 210), Tertullian denied the possibility of post-baptismal reconciliation for serious sinners. He held that the grave sins of idolatry, adultery, and murder were outside of the church's power of reconciliation, and those who committed these sins were permanently excluded from communion.[77] The treatise was occasioned by the innovative practice of a bishop to allow those guilty of adultery to be admitted to public penance and to gain pardon and readmission to communion.[78] Tertullian argued that the sins of adultery and fornication were always beyond the authority of the church to forgive.[79] Those who were guilty could not be granted readmission to eucharistic communion, but they were exhorted to repent and to seek the support of intercessory prayers from the community. Their only hope for forgiveness was God's mercy at the final judgment.[80] Sins such as incest and blasphemy resulted in permanent excommunication and expulsion from the community.[81]

The administration of the sacraments was normally performed by the clergy, but the power to confer the sacraments belonged to the whole church as the body of Christ. Tertullian identified three clerical orders of bishop, presbyter, and deacon. The bishop celebrated baptism, eucharistic worship, and reconciliation, and he was responsible for teaching true doctrine. The succession of bishops from the apostles preserved continuity in doctrine and right interpretation, but Tertullian did not identify the twelve as bishops.[82] The distinction between *ordo* and *plebs* allowed for the best administration of the church, but Tertullian held to the universal priesthood of believers. Tertullian argued that sacramental powers were granted to the church as a whole, not solely the clergy, although in practice they were exercised in public assemblies by designated males. However, male Christians were able to perform baptism in emergency or preside at prayer or Eucharist in private gatherings.[83] The martyrs were a special class within the church, and Tertullian also recognized the prophets as a distinctive non-clerical group. The spiritual ones manifested charismatic gifts, such as seeing visions during the liturgy and performing miracles. The gifts of the Holy Spirit belonged to the whole community, not merely the clergy, and all Christians received the Holy Spirit by means of the sacraments.[84] While the clergy typically administered the sacraments, the source of their power came from the whole church as the body of Christ. Yet not even the whole church could forgive grave sins, for this belonged to God alone.

By the third century, the church in North Africa had begun to take definitive shape, and it was based on a theology that focused on the church as the medium of Christ's salvific work.[85] The church was the continuing presence of Christ on earth, mediating Christ and the Spirit by its rituals. The church was one and holy because of the presence and activity of Christ and the Spirit. Those who shared in the sacraments were granted a share in the church's unity in charity. Those who committed serious sins after baptism were cut off from the Spirit, and in Tertullian's determination, they were not permitted to return. Only God could forgive certain sins, and the presence of sinners polluted the church. In order to understand how Tertullian came to this conclusion, let us examine the development of his ecclesiology.

TERTULLIAN'S THOUGHT

Before looking at Tertullian's understanding of the church, a brief discussion of the most influential sources on his thought is necessary. As we have seen, Tertullian was trained in Greco-Roman rhetoric and was influenced by philosophy, particularly Stoicism.[86] While philosophy could be used to support idolatry and heresy, Tertullian held that Christianity contained the truth in all simplicity based upon divine revelation.[87] In Tertullian's view, Christianity was the better philosophy.[88] Philosophy was a useful tool for the explanation of truth revealed in Christianity.

Tertullian's theology developed from his interpretation of the Scriptures and the tradition. The Scriptures were authoritative and belonged to the church, not to heretics who had no right to use them.[89] Since the faith existed before the written record, the validity of the Scriptures depended upon conformity to the rule of faith (*regula fidei*).[90] The rule of faith also served as the criterion for the proper interpretation of the Scriptures. Tertullian maintained a priority of tradition over Scripture, for Scripture was a record of tradition.[91] Tertullian espoused belief in the simplicity of Scripture, such that apparent inconsistencies could be explained, but this did not mean that the Scriptures were unsophisticated or could be understood based upon a singular mode of interpretation. Indeed, Tertullian used multiple approaches to interpret Scripture, arguing for spiritual, allegorical, or typological interpretations of certain passages while advocating a more literal interpretation of others.

Tertullian was not a systematic theologian, and it is important to remember that he wrote from a rhetorical perspective. This means that his views were ambiguous at times, and he advocated some positions in order to prove particular points. This was typical of many patristic authors, and in order to grasp their complex thinking, it is necessary to pay attention to the context, audience, and interrelation of primary sources.[92]

Scholars have recently drawn attention to the significance of Tertullian's African identity upon his thought.[93] For instance, Tertullian's self-awareness as an African was evident in his wearing of the cloak or pallium rather than the Roman toga, in claiming Africa as his *patria* or homeland, and in his solidarity with Africans over against Roman political colonization and religious persecution.[94] Along these lines, it is important to consider the impact indigenous African religions had upon Tertullian and African Christianity as a whole. As we have seen, Tertullian and North Africans lived in a religiously diverse context. This did not have the effect of diminishing religious devotion, but rather it spurred commitment to one's distinctive religious identity. For instance, some scholars have suggested that the African Christian martyrs' willingness to die for their faith might owe something to the indigenous practices of self-sacrifice among earlier Punic religious cults.[95] The fact that human sacrifices were made to Baal in ancient Carthage most certainly impacted Christian reflection upon the meaning of sacrifice, although Christians like Tertullian would redefine sacrifice not only in terms of martyrdom, but also in terms of the sacrifice of Christ. Christian liturgical practice mediated the sacrifice of Christ and constituted the offering of the whole Christian church.[96] Christian sacrifice was multi-layered and included not only a share in the historical sacrifice of Christ on the cross but also included the prayers of the church on earth, the sharing of the eucharistic meal, and the works of mercy offered to the poor. While Christianity developed distinct teachings and practices, at the very least, the religious devotion of North African religions influenced Christian devotion and commitment to the faith, even to the point of death.

Tertullian's thought grew in the context of major theological debates with perceived heretical Christian groups in North Africa such as Monarchians, Marcionites, Valentinian Gnostics, and Novatianists. Tertullian also focused attacks on heretical teachers such as Marcion, Hermogenes, and Praxeas. In some of his works, Tertullian engaged in polemics against the Jews. There was a Jewish presence in North Africa dating back at least to the second century,[97] but by the year 200, Jews were only a small community at Carthage.[98] Tertullian's treatise *Against the Jews* has been used to argue that perhaps he had some form of contact with Jews in North Africa.[99] Like other Christians, Tertullian engaged in debates over whether contemporary Judaism had legitimate claims to ongoing identity. Tertullian argued that Christians inherited Jewish claims to being an ancient religion.[100] Scholars remain uncertain about the extent to which Tertullian's statements against the Jews can be perceived as inflammatory rhetoric, as something symbolic to help Christian self-understanding, and/or as evidence of real historical contact with Jewish communities.[101]

Around 206, Tertullian became attracted to Montanism, a prophetic movement that originated in Phrygia in the late second century.[102] The followers of the New Prophecy in Phrygia were only later called Montanists after their apparent leader, Montanus, and it is clear that Tertullian never met a Phrygian prophet in person and only knew of them through their recorded sayings. Montanism was a "prophetic renewal movement informed by the Holy Spirit," and it could be characterized as charismatic, ascetic, enthusiastic, innovative, spiritualist, ecstatic and rigorous.[103] Montanists claimed to be inspired by the Paraclete, which could place them in opposition to the authority of the bishops. They were considered to be elitist because of their demanding and perfectionist views of Christian life, as they insisted on rigorous fasting, forbade remarriage, and did not believe in post-baptismal reconciliation of sinners. As discussed earlier, scholars have rejected the idea that Tertullian left the church of Carthage to join a schismatic group called the Montanists,[104] yet it is evident that he was influenced by his exposure to the sources of the New Prophecy. Like the Phrygian prophets, Tertullian identified spiritual (*spiritalis*) Christians in opposition to carnal or fleshly (*carnalis*) ones.[105] Following Paul's language, Tertullian began to speak of his opponents as unspiritual or *psychichi*, a transliteration for the Greek word for soul (*psyche*), which is lower than the spirit.[106] Beyond this shift, there are no significant signs of change in Tertullian's views on the practice of Christianity, for even his teachings on marriage, which are sometimes attributed to his Montanism, can be found in his earlier works on the subject.[107] Indeed, as Geoffrey Dunn has argued, there is much that is Montanist in virtually all of Tertullian's writings, even before his so-called Montanist period, and Dunn is not inclined to see two distinct phases in Tertullian's literary life.[108] This does not mean that there is no development in Tertullian's thought, but it is an argument in favor of the consistency and continuity between his earlier works and later writings.

TERTULLIAN'S WORKS

Tertullian's extant works span from 196–212 and consist of 31 treatises, which can be classified according to four categories: 1) apologetics, 2) exhortations, 3) polemics, and 4) polemical exhortations.[109] These works were addressed to particular audiences, although it is not always clear what these audiences were and if the works were delivered to the intended audiences. It is important to examine his writings in their particular contexts to the extent possible, and to remember that Tertullian was a master rhetorician who often assumed opposite positions in order to suit his aims. For instance, in his work to the African consul *To Scapula* (c. 212), Tertullian asserted that Christians were not a threat to the Roman Empire, which would continue as God had ordained,[110] whereas in *To the Nations* (c. 197), Tertullian wrote to his local Carthaginians that the Roman Empire was bound to come to an apocalyptic end.[111] Tertullian's understanding of the church, like his theology as a whole, is notoriously difficult to grasp. In order to do so, let us keep in mind his rhetorical aims, his immediate ecclesial concerns, and his interpretation of the Scriptures.

TERTULLIAN ON THE CHURCH

What precisely is the church (*ecclesia*), according to Tertullian? In some instances, Tertullian used *ecclesia* to refer to the Christian community, constituted by the hierarchy (bishops, priests, and deacons) and all who have been baptized and participate in sacramental worship.[112] In other cases, Tertullian suggested that the church might include those who have not yet joined the visible community but have the Spirit. Catechumens who have been persecuted and imprisoned present a unique case. Although Tertullian did not explicitly call unbaptized catechumens members of the church, he argued that the Spirit resided with the imprisoned, and that catechumens who endured martyrdom would undergo baptism by blood.[113] In the exhortation *To the Martyrs* (c. 197), which was addressed to the imprisoned, Tertullian wrote that "mother church (*mater ecclesia*)" provided for the bodily and spiritual needs of those held captive.[114] He distinguished between the visible community that provided material support and the work of the Holy Spirit to offer spiritual nourishment. Tertullian sought to encourage the imprisoned by noting that the martyrs possessed the peace of the Lord and the peace of the kingdom, which was at war with the kingdom of the devil.[115] Some Christians sought the Lord's peace from the imprisoned since they were unable to find it in the visible church.[116] Tertullian thus introduced a distinction between the visible ecclesial community and those who had not yet been baptized but had received the gifts of the Spirit.

In the same work, Tertullian asserted that Christians who were held captive and remained open to the Spirit rather than the lusts of the world may gain more than they might lose in the flesh.[117] They were outside of the church, but they were able to receive the Spirit. In this context Tertullian made his famous declaration that Christians are in the world, but not of it,[118] for while the brethren provided for the needs of the flesh (*caro*), the Spirit obtained greater benefits of faith.[119] Thus, it was better to be in prison than to be worldly.[120] In Tertullian's early works, there developed a tension between the visible, ecclesial community and the invisible work of the Spirit. To be sure, that did not render the visible community unnecessary, nor did it mean that Christians need not participate in the sacramental life of the church. However, Tertullian placed primacy upon the presence and gifts of the Holy Spirit in order to determine ecclesial membership. Not only did the Spirit work beyond empirical limits, but those clergy and laity within the church had to demonstrate holiness of life and detachment from sin in order to be considered true members. Tertullian's use of Biblical images for the church revealed his growing emphasis upon the presence and activity of the Spirit as the necessary criteria for membership in the church.

IMAGES OF THE CHURCH

Tertullian used figures and images from the Scriptures in order to show that the church was the work of God with its origin in the Trinity. In his polemical work *Against the Jews* (c. 197), Tertullian claimed that the figures of the Hebrew Scriptures foreshadowed the church. The church was the spiritual temple that was prefigured by the Jewish temple.[121] The Lord works to build the church as God's temple, the holy city, and the house of the Lord.[122] The church's origin and identity can be traced to the one, Triune God of Christianity. In the exhortation *On Prayer* (c. 198), Tertullian asserted that God the Father has begotten many sons, as prophesied in Isaiah 1:2 and attested by the Holy Spirit.[123] By calling God Father, the Son was invoked, for the Son declared "I and the Father are one" in John 10:30.[124] Those who have God as Father are born of the church as mother.[125] Christians were defined by their relation to the Father, Son, and Holy Spirit. One must have the Spirit to pray properly while remaining free from sin, for a defiled spirit could not be acknowledged by the Holy Spirit (Eph. 4:30).[126] In Tertullian's view, Christians were not only required to believe the proper doctrine in order to be members of the church. Tertullian went further by arguing that if one did not profess Christ as one with the Father, one could not have the Spirit, and thus one could not be born from the church as mother.

The profession of faith was required prior to the reception of the ritual of baptism. Baptism was a rebirth due to the work of the Triune God. In the treatise *On Baptism* (c. 198), Tertullian laid out his teaching on the sacrament of baptism. The Trinity, invoked by the baptismal formula, worked through the washing of water in order to cleanse sins, to grant faith, and to prepare the way for the sending of the Spirit.[127] The Spirit was then offered by the imposition of hands. Tertullian remarked that in the ritual celebration of baptism, the church was mentioned by necessity, for wherever the three persons of the Trinity are, there is the church, a body of three.[128] While this was not a simple identification of the Trinity and the church, Tertullian strongly associated the church with the three persons of the Trinity. According to Tertullian, the church's unity was grounded in the unity of the one Triune God, for there is one church just as there is one God, following Ephesians 4:4–6.[129] The Triune God was the pattern and the source of the church's life.

Tertullian continued to associate the church with the persons of the Trinity in his exhortation *On Penance*, composed around the same time as *On Baptism* (c. 198). The church was the body of Christ, and in the company of two Christians, Christ was present (Matt. 18:20).[130] The church truly *is* Christ (*ecclesia uero Christus*),[131] for when one entreats another, one is entreating Christ, and when one sheds tears, it is Christ who suffers and Christ who prays.[132] The church is the body of Christ offering forgiveness and interceding on behalf of the members.[133] Where Christ is present, there is the church.[134]

Likewise, Tertullian identified the church with the presence of the Holy Spirit. In the polemical exhortation *On Modesty* (c. 210), Tertullian focused on the church's role in the remission of sins. Here Tertullian made his clearest argument that serious sins could not be forgiven by the church, for not even Peter, who had been given the power to bind and to loosen by Christ in John 20:22–23, could forgive grave sins. In this text, Tertullian interpreted Peter as a figure of the spiritual person who has the power to forgive. Peter represented all of the spiritual members of the body, not merely the episcopal office. While the clergy remained the ministers of the sacrament of reconciliation, it was the church of the Spirit that forgave sins. "The church, it is true, will forgive sins: but [it will be] the church of the Spirit, by means of a spiritual man; not the church which consists of a number of bishops."[135] In this context, Tertullian declared that "the church is itself properly and principally the Spirit, in whom is the Trinity of One Divinity–Father, Son, and Holy Spirit. The Spirit brings together that church which the Lord has set down in three."[136] One cannot have the church without the Spirit, for the Spirit unites the many members of the church as one. However, the church could not forgive grave sins such as fornication and adultery because these sins were directed against God.[137] God alone could forgive such sins, and this was reserved for final judgment, either at death or at the second coming of Christ. In the meantime, the apostle Paul indicated that those who were guilty of such sins must be given over to Satan for the destruction of the flesh (1 Cor. 5:5).[138] These sins were worthy of condemnation, and the guilty had to be expelled from the church.

Tertullian used other Biblical images in order to set firm boundaries around the church as a spiritual reality free from the impurity of sin. For instance, Tertullian spoke of the church as God's threshing floor, where the grain had been separated from the chaff (Matt. 3:12).[139] Whereas later theologians like Augustine argued that such a separation would come at the end time, Tertullian believed that God's judgment was already taking place in the midst of persecution. God separated the grain of the believers and the martyrs from the chaff of the apostates. In his moral exhortation *On Monogamy* (c. 210), Tertullian declared that the church, as the spouse of Christ, cannot commit adultery but must be monogamous in spirit after the example of Christ.[140] The church must be in the flesh what Christ was in the spirit. Only those who reject sin and live moral lives, as embodied by the practice of monogamy, could be spiritual members of the church rather than animal members of Adam (1 Cor. 15:46). God will pass judgment on what has been done in the body, and in order to enter into heaven, one must be cleansed from all filth of flesh and spirit (2 Cor. 7:1) and be espoused to Christ as a chaste virgin (2 Cor. 11:2).[141] Christians must be holy in the flesh, for Christ assumed true human flesh and was born in the flesh while also being born of the Spirit.[142] The flesh has received the sacraments but the soul is illuminated by the Spirit, and the flesh feeds on the body and blood of Christ so that the soul may feed on God.[143] To be a member of the church meant to be pure in body and in spirit, and thus it was necessary to reject sexual immorality, as well as spiritual adultery in the form of idolatry.

Further, to be a member of the church meant to be engaged in war with the kingdom of the devil while enjoying the peace of God. The world was antithetical to the church, for the world represented the delights of the flesh while the church enjoyed spiritual delights.[144] The serpent in Genesis was the devil who sought to crush human beings to death. The devil and his demons continued to make war with the church by means of the pagan idols.[145] The church was the camp of light at war with the army of pagan darkness.[146] The church was the house and the city of God prefigured in the Old Testament.[147] Jacob was a type of the church by seeking a heavenly blessing, while Esau sought an earthly one.[148] Noah's ark was a figure of the holy church free from the pollution of sin. The waters signified baptism and the cleansing from sin. The dove that returned with the olive branch offered a token of peace after the flood. So too after baptism, the dove of the Holy Spirit was sent from heaven to bring the peace of God to the pure church.[149] These images allowed Tertullian to establish clear boundaries around the church, and to maintain elevated criteria for membership. Above all, membership in the church required reception of the Holy Spirit, who offered the gifts of peace, unity, and charity to the members. Those who committed serious sins did not have the Spirit. They had to be removed from the community and could not be readmitted. All Christians who had received the Spirit had to manifest the Spirit's presence by holy living.[150] Tertullian recognized that the Spirit gave some members of the church special gifts or charisms. They included the laity and most notably women.

SPIRITUAL GIFTS

Tertullian's writings offer testimony to the presence of charismatic gifts among the members of the church of Carthage in the third century. In *Against the Jews*, Tertullian claimed that the Holy Spirit worked among the Israelites by means of the prophets to predict the spiritual sacrifices offered to God in the church.[151] The Holy Spirit has continued to work in the church by granting the gifts of prophecy, visions, and other spiritual charisms to the members of the body.[152] Tertullian mentioned one particular woman in the church who experienced ecstatic visions and heard mysterious communications while participating in the sacred rites, that is, during liturgical worship. She could understand the hearts of others, and she could offer healing remedies by the gift of the Holy Spirit. Such prophetic visions and gifts of healing were accepted within Tertullian's community in Carthage, for they were foretold by Paul (1 Cor. 12).[153] Tertullian observed that the woman who was given spiritual gifts during the liturgy regularly reported her visions to be examined by the church.[154] Thus, the special gifts and private revelations experienced by the members of the church in Carthage were subject to scrutiny by the local ecclesial leaders.

In *Against Marcion* (c. 208), Tertullian asserted that women have spiritual gifts, especially prophecy, while heretics like Marcion wrongly attempted to silence such women in the church.[155] Tertullian established three criteria for prophecy of the Spirit according to rule of grace. This gift was intended to: 1) foretell the future, 2) reveal the secrets of the heart, and 3) explain mysteries.[156] Marcion's community, however, did not have the Spirit, as evident in their doctrine and by their way of life, nor did they possess true prophecy.[157] There was only one church, the church constituted by proper belief, practice, and spiritual gifts.

In Tertullian's theology, the church's unity in charity by the gift of the Spirit meant that there could be no pollution due to sin. This was a claim about the nature of the Spirit, for the Spirit could not tolerate evil or sin. Baptism was a cleansing of sins that prepared the way for the Spirit.[158] With the sending of the Spirit by the imposition of hands, the gifts of charity and peace were distributed among the members in order to bind them together. Charity must be manifested by deeds of love, including almsgiving and care for the needy in the one Spirit of holiness.[159] All Christians must demonstrate charity as a sign of the Spirit, whether or not they possessed special gifts such as prophecy. In his exhortation *On Patience* (c. 198), Tertullian taught that charity should also be manifested in forgiveness, yet he asserted that patience was shown in order to lead sinners to repentance. Charity was long-suffering because it was patient, but patience did no evil,[160] therefore, there could be no evil where there was patience and charity. Evil brought death, and the deadly sins (1 John 5:16) such as adultery, fornication, idolatry, murder, and incest were monstrosities that could send souls to hell.[161] Those who committed such monstrosities must be given over to Satan for the destruction of the flesh (1 Cor. 5:5).[162] While some had argued that God would forgive because God is good, Tertullian declared that God is just too, and in God, there can be no evil.[163] The church must be purified by the expulsion of sinners. Persecution helped to reveal and separate the grain from the chaff, the saints from the sinners, the martyrs from the apostates. In Tertullian's view, sinners had cut themselves off from Christ and the Holy Spirit,[164] and ultimately, the church was constituted solely by the spiritual members united in charity.

According to Tertullian, the presence and activity of the Holy Spirit were the primary criterion for membership in the church. However, in his works, he also accounted for the church's visible, empirical form as an institution constituted by clergy and laity spread throughout the world. The visible church was united in its adherence to the true doctrine received from Christ by the apostles and preserved by the apostolic succession of the bishops. Unity with the bishops was a necessary but not sufficient condition for union with the invisible body of Christ. The bishops served as visible signs of union of the universal (*catholica*) church. Thus, although Tertullian did not explicitly identify four distinguishing marks for the church, they are evident in his ecclesiology: the church is only, holy, catholic, and apostolic.[165] In Tertullian's thought, the church's apostolic unity was subordinated to its invisible union in charity.

THE APOSTOLIC CHURCH

In works from the early 200s, Tertullian held in tension the ecclesial authority of the apostolic church with the work of the Holy Spirit. In his polemical work *Prescript Against the Heretics* (c. 203), Tertullian established the authority of the hierarchy based upon the authority of the apostles. As the ones chosen by Christ and sent to baptize, the apostles founded churches and obtained the power of the Holy Spirit.[166] The apostles founded churches throughout the world, and all churches were offspring of apostolic churches.[167] There was only one primitive church, from which all others spring.[168] The church was founded by Christ and built upon Peter as the rock (Matt. 16:18).[169] According to Tertullian, Peter served as a sign of the union of the whole church. The bishop of Rome exercised his authority by preserving doctrine, and his episcopal see possessed an elevated status because of the blood of Peter and Paul.[170] Christ left the keys of the kingdom to Peter,[171] who was given the power of binding and loosening sins. Nevertheless, not even Peter could forgive capital sins.[172] As we have seen, the power to forgive sins belonged to the spiritual in the church rather than exclusively to the clergy. At the same time, Tertullian asserted that the apostles were given unique spiritual gifts of miracles, prophecy and utterance.[173] These gifts redounded to all of the spiritual members of the church. As successors of the apostles, the bishops were entrusted with the mission of teaching and handing on true doctrine. The apostles received the truth from Christ, and Christ from God, and this truth was handed on to all apostolic churches.[174] Unity in doctrine had its ultimate source in God, and communion with the apostolic church meant unity in the teaching received from and preached by the apostles.[175] Heretics lacked this unity because of their diverse and erroneous teachings.[176] As Tertullian declared, where God is, there is the truth, and there is a united church.[177]

In the book of Acts, the Holy Spirit came down upon the apostles in order to lead them into truth.[178] Tertullian claimed that the heretics rejected this sending of the Spirit and thus could not claim to be a church. Christ sent the Holy Spirit to lead the apostles into truth, and the rule of faith (*regula fidei*) has been preserved and handed on by the preaching of the apostles.[179] Any community that would claim to be a church must demonstrate apostolic succession, that is, the ordination of bishops from the apostolic lineage.[180] Apostolic churches not only possessed authentic writings but also authentic preaching,[181] as well as authority over customs and practices, such as the sacred rites and the practice of the veiling of virgins. For there was "one faith for us and for them, one God, the same Christ, the same hope, the same mysteries of the ritual bath, let me say once for all, we are one church."[182] Rome was pre-eminent and possessed the very authority of the apostles because of the doctrine it received, the authority given to Peter, and the blood poured out by Peter and Paul as martyrs.[183] Heretics like Marcion and Valentinus were once believers of the doctrine of the Catholic Church of Rome,[184] but they have strayed by their erroneous teachings and now wander without belonging to any church.[185] The Holy Spirit was at work to guide the church in truth,[186] but heretics have cut themselves off from the truth about God preserved by the church.

Tertullian's understanding of episcopal authority came from his view of the Holy Spirit's role as the guarantor of truth. The church's unity in doctrine came from the work of the Spirit to guide the apostles and the succession of bishops. Further, the offices of bishop, presbyter, and deacon possessed the authority to lead the celebration of the sacraments.[187] Yet Tertullian maintained that the power and operation of the Holy Spirit need not be associated with an ecclesiastical office. The Holy Spirit was present and active in the church among clergy and laity as revealed by the gifts of prophecy, visions, and healing.[188] Thus, while the episcopal office was entrusted with preserving unity in doctrine and practice by tracing its lineage to the apostles, this unity was not a monopoly on the Spirit. In fact, any member of the church could fall into serious sin, including bishops. Only the spiritual ones could claim membership in the church. Tertullian gave primacy to the invisible work of charity over the visible unity enjoyed by the episcopal college. That being said, Tertullian thought that the visible church served as the normal means of the mediation of holiness and salvation to the world.

NO SALVATION OUTSIDE OF THE CHURCH

Tertullian did not provide a systematic soteriology that accounted for the possible salvation of people outside of the church. He did consider the status of the Jewish people, but he was more concerned with arguing for the truth of Christianity against Judaism. Tertullian often argued rhetorically against the Jews in order to instruct Christians and to help define the church.[189] He understood the Mosaic law as a preparation for the Gospel, and the faith of the ancient ones was an anticipation of faith in Christ. Tertullian firmly argued that Christians need not keep the law and the sabbath, for they do not provide justification.[190] However, the keeping of the sabbath and rituals such as circumcision enabled the holy ones to be friends of God.[191] Tertullian argued that God praised Abel as he offered sacrifice, even though he was not circumcised and did not keep sabbath.[192] The same could be said about Noah, Enoch, Melchizedek, and Lot, who lived upright lives.[193] The figures and events of the Old Testament prefigured the salvation brought about by Christ.[194] After Christ's coming, those Jews who refused to recognize him would lose what they had been given, for the grace of God had ceased among them.[195] The church, which consisted of the holy priests of the spiritual temple, would enjoy a feast of the Lord's grace, while those who failed to recognize him would remain without a taste of salvation.[196] The invitation to salvation has been offered to the Gentiles and to all nations, for "Christ extended to all men the law of his Father's compassion, excepting none from his mercy as he omitted none in his invitation."[197] This could hardly be interpreted as a declaration of universal salvation, for Tertullian was clear that those who committed deadly sins warranted the punishment of hell.[198] Tertullian did not elaborate on the operation of grace among the elect, although he maintained that human beings were free to do what God commanded or not.[199] His concern was to show that Christ's mission applied to all nations, not merely Israel, and this mission was accomplished by means of the church.

In Tertullian's thought, there could be no salvation outside of Christ, and there was no salvation outside of the one church. In order to be a member of the church, one not only had to affirm the true doctrine received and preserved by apostolic succession, one also had to receive the sacraments and observe the moral tenets and practices of the faith. If a Christian committed grave sin, she was cut off from the church and could not be readmitted. Tertullian exhorted such a person to repent, perform penance, ask for intercession, and hope for God's mercy. But the church must be a virgin free from all stain of sin.[200] The church was composed of saints, not sinners.[201] The church could not tolerate the impurity and contagion of sin. The church could only be found where the Spirit was found. Tertullian maintained a high standard of conduct for Christians that marked African Christianity in Carthage until at least the fourth century.[202]

CONCLUSION

As the first Latin theologian of Christianity, Tertullian held a doctrine of the church that was defined by the presence and work of the Triune God. According to Tertullian, the church's unity and holiness come from the Trinity. Just as the Trinity is three yet one, so too the church has many members but is one. Tertullian associated the church's holiness with Christ and the Holy Spirit, such that where Christ and the Spirit are present, there is the church. The church is one and holy because God is one and holy.

Tertullian gave priority to the Holy Spirit's work to unite the members in charity and peace. This unity was evident in the charitable works shown toward one's neighbors, and in the special gifts given to certain spiritual members, such as visions, prophetic utterings, and miraculous healings. The members of the church were also obligated to adhere to a clear ethical code of conduct, and to practice spiritual disciplines such as prayer, fasting, and almsgiving. Since the church was constituted primarily by the presence and activity of the Holy Spirit, there was no room for sin in the church. Sin was antithetical to the Spirit, and anyone who lived in sin was not part of the one dove. Those who committed grave sins such as idolatry, adultery, and murder cut themselves off from the church permanently. The church did not have the power to forgive such sins, for only God could spare them on judgment day.

Due to these theological commitments, Tertullian refused to readmit those guilty of serious sins to the church. Idolatry was a kind of contagion that had to be kept outside of the holy church. The chaff had to be separated from the grain, and persecution prompted the purification of apostates from the church. The church's leaders were responsible for preserving and protecting the church's purity, not only by handing on and teaching true doctrine, but also by keeping sinners out of the fold. The church's holiness had to be safeguarded from the impurity of sin. Tertullian advocated strict adherence to the Christian code of conduct. Only those who maintained holy living could be considered members of the church. Underlying this view was his understanding of the church as the presence of the Triune God in the world, particularly the presence of the Spirit, who was alive and active in the members. The spiritual ones gave evidence of the Spirit by moral conduct, charity, and charismatics gifts. Although the clergy possessed distinctive roles in the administration of the sacraments and the preservation of doctrine, they were not thereby guaranteed participation in the Spirit. They could cut themselves off by committing serious sins just like the laity. Tertullian was adamant that such sinners had forfeited their membership. Thus, Tertullian's doctrine of the church depended heavily upon the moral condition of the members, for the church had to remain free from the pollution of sin. Sinners had to be excluded in order to maintain the pristine purity of the church. Tertullian's ecclesiology can rightly be described as exclusionist, perfectionist, and rigorist.

Tertullian faced some opposition to his views, and his position on the readmission of sinners remained controversial. Even during his lifetime, bishops in North Africa had begun seeking ways to readmit the lapsed, much to Tertullian's dismay. Cyprian sought to retain much of the tradition he received from the church in Carthage, but he was also persuaded by his episcopal colleagues to consider a more moderate approach toward reconciling sinners. Behind this change in practice was an ecclesiology that prioritized the bishop's power to forgive sins and to restore sinners to the charity of the church. Like Tertullian, Cyprian developed an ecclesiology characterized by the four marks of the church as one, holy, catholic, and apostolic. However, Cyprian emphasized the church's unity around the bishop to the extent that the bishop could forgive any sin and determine the proper penitential process to readmit sinners into the fold. This emphasis upon the bishops grounded his famous declaration that outside of the church, there is no salvation. Contrary to Tertullian, Cyprian argued that the Holy Spirit belonged to the episcopacy in definitive fashion, such that the church was essentially constituted by unity around the episcopal college. Thus, Cyprian offered a new way of looking at the church's unity in charity.

NOTES

1. Tertullian, *Mart.* 2.5; CCSL 1.4: "ubi sitis in saeculo, qui extra saeculum estis."
2. See the discussion by Wilhite, *Ancient African Christianity*, 112–14.
3. Dunn, *Tertullian*, 3. The classic biography is Timothy Barnes, *Tertullian: A Historical and Literary Study* (Oxford: Oxford University Press, 1985).
4. Wilhite, *Ancient African Christianity*, 115; Dunn, *Tertullian*, 5; Barnes, *Tertullian*, 196–206.
5. Wilhite, *Ancient African Christianity*, 109; Dunn, *Tertullian*, 4.
6. Perhaps Tertullian witnessed martyrdom; Tertullian, *Paen.* 1.1; *Fug.* 6.2.
7. Wilhite, *Ancient African Christianity*, 112; Tertullian, *Apol.* 18.4; 50.15; *Paen.* 1.1; *Scap.* 5.5; *Carn. Chr.* 59.3; *Pat.* 1.1; *Mon.* 12.2; *Cast.* 7.3. Tertullian's claim to priesthood in *Ieiun.* 11.4 appears to be the claim to the universal priesthood of all Christian believers (1 Pet. 2:9); Dunn, *Tertullian*, 5.
8. Jane Merdinger, "Roman North Africa," in William Tabbernee (ed.), *Early Christianity in Contexts: An Exploration across Cultures and Continents* (Grand Rapids: Baker Academic, 2014), 234.
9. Tertullian, *Ux.* 1.6.1; Tertullian confessed to adultery in *Res.* 59.3.
10. Wilhite, *Ancient African Christianity*, 109.
11. Dunn, *Tertullian*, 5.
12. Merdinger, "Roman North Africa," 229.
13. Fracois Decret, *Early Christianity in North Africa*, trans. Edward L. Smither (Eugene: Cascade), 4.
14. Wilhite, *Ancient African Christianity*, 45–78, 116.
15. Wilhite, *Ancient African Christianity*, 14–15, 45–67.
16. In order to understand what is "African" about Tertullian, see Wilhite, *Ancient African Christianity*, 116–28; David Wilhite, *Tertullian the African: An Anthropological Reading of Tertullian's Context and Identities* (Berlin: Walter De Gruyter, 2007).
17. Wilhite, *Ancient African Christianity*, 116.
18. See the discussion in Wilhite, *Ancient African Christianity*, 47–49, and 115–16. Wilhite notes that Tertullian coined the term *Romanitas*, but he did so while mocking Roman-ness (Wilhite, 115); see also Éric Rebillard, *Christians and Their Many Identities in Late Antiquity, North Africa, 200–450 CE* (Ithaca: Cornell University Press, 2012).
19. Decret, *Early Christianity in North Africa*, 12–15; Dunn, *Tertullian*, 14–15, Merdinger, "Roman North Africa," 223–43.
20. Decret, *Early Christianity in North Africa*, 9.
21. Burns, Jensen, et al., *Christianity in Roman Africa*, 4.
22. Wilhite, *Ancient African Christianity*, 15.
23. Decret, *Early Christianity in North Africa*, 11.
24. Wilhite, *Ancient African Christianity*, 58; Burns, Jensen, et al., *Christianity in Roman Africa*, 491–517; Stephen E. Potthoff, *The Afterlife in Early Christian Carthage: Near-Death Experience, Ancestor Cult, and the Archaeology of Paradise* (New York: Routledge, 2017). On burial sites in the fourth and fifth centuries in North Africa, see Shira Lander, *Ritual Sites and Religious Rivalries in Late Roman North Africa* (Cambridge: Cambridge University Press, 2016).

25. Decret, *Early Christianity in North Africa*, 11. Decret concludes that there was likely a church in Carthage before the end of the first century. Wilhite, however, asserts that there is no evidence to corroborate a first-century dating for Christianity in the African provinces, although he acknowledges the case for Cyrenaica; see Wilhite, *Ancient African Christianity*, 82; Thomas Oden, *Early Libyan Christianity: Uncovering a North African Tradition* (Downers Grove: Intervarsity Press, 2011), 214–42. In any case, it is likely that some Christians had reached Africa a half-century or more before the report of the Scillitan martyrs; Burns, Jensen, et al., *Christianity in Roman Africa*, 4.

26. Wilhite, *Ancient African Christianity*, 87–88.

27. Wilhite, *Ancient African Christianity*, 88; Thomas J. Heffernan, *The Passion of Perpetua and Felicity* (Oxford: Oxford University Press, 2012), 33.

28. Heffernan, *The Passion*, 33n35.

29. Merdinger, "Roman North Africa," 231.

30. *Pas. Perp.* 6.4. With pagan rites and symbols permeating every aspect of civic life, the ancient world knew no distinction between religion and the state; Merdinger, "Roman North Africa," 232.

31. Wilhite, *Ancient African Christianity*, 62–65.

32. Wilhite, *Ancient African Christianity*, 94; cf. Christine Trevett, *Montanism: Gender, Authority and the New Prophecy* (Cambridge: Cambridge University Press, 1996), 69–70.

33. Burns, Jensen, et al., *Christianity in Roman Africa*, 4–5.

34. Dunn, *Tertullian*, 5. Heffernan concludes that by the first decade of the third century, the Christian population amounted to about fifteen hundred, or 0.5 percent of the population; Heffernan, *The Passion of Perpetua*, 246. Some estimates have ranged up to 70,000 Christians in the second century; see Rebillard, *Christians and Their Many Identities*, 10.

35. Tertullian, *Prax.* 3.1.; Dunn, *Tertullian*, 5. If only 10 percent of the population was literate, and Christians accounted for 0.35 percent of the population of 700,000 in Carthage, that would mean that only some 245 Christians were literate in the year 200; Dunn places it at 230, while noting that the number could be significantly less if the population of Carthage was smaller; Dunn, 5.

36. Tertullian, *Scap.* 2.10; 3–4; *Mon.* 12.3; Burns, Jensen, et al., *Christianity in Roman Africa*, 4.

37. Burns, Jensen, et al., *Christianity in Roman Africa*, 5.

38. Wilhite, *Ancient African Christianity*, 121.

39. Burns, Jensen, et al., *Christianity in Roman Africa*, 167.

40. Tertullian, *Spec.* 8.9–10.

41. Eric Osborn, *Tertullian: First Theologian of the West* (New York: Cambridge University Press, 1997), 183–91.

42. Tertullian, *Pud.* 9.8–15; *Ieiun.* 2.3–5, 8.3; *Mon.* 2.1–3.

43. Tertullian, *Bapt.* 4; 6.

44. Burns, Jensen, et al., *Christianity in Roman Africa*, 167.

45. Tertullian, *Bapt.* 15; *Pud.* 19.5.

46. Tertullian, *Bapt.* 18.

47. Tertullian did not think that infants or children had to be baptized since infants had no sins to be forgiven, yet this argument gives indirect evidence that Christians in North Africa were baptizing infants and young children; Tertullian, *Bapt.* 18.

48. Tertullian, *Bapt.* 5.

49. Tertullian, *Bapt.* 4.

50. Tertullian, *Bapt.* 4–6.

51. Tertullian, *Cor.* 3.3.

52. Tertullian, *Bapt.* 17.

53. Tertullian, *Bapt.* 12; 15; *Pud.* 19.5.

54. Tertullian, *Bapt.* 16.

55. Burns, Jensen, et al., *Christianity in Roman Africa*, 233.

56. Tertullian, *Apol.* 39.16.

57. Tertullian, *Or.* 19.1–4; *Cor.* 3.3.

58. Tertullian, *Or.* 1.

59. Tertullian only uses the term *eucharistia* seven times in his extant works, but nonetheless, he offers a rich eucharistic theology; cf. *Or.* 19.1–2; *Cor.* 3.3; *Praesc.* 36.5; *Pud.* 9.16, 18.8; *Or.* 24; *Marc.* 4.34.5.

60. Tertullian, *Marc.* 3.19.4; 4.40.3–6; 5.8.3.

61. Tertullian, *Spec.* 13.4; 25.5; *Idol.* 7.

62. Tertullian, *Pud.* 13.10–12; 14.17; 15.3, 9–11; 18.2, 8, 12–18; 14–16.

63. Tertullian, *Pud.* 5.

64. Tertullian, *Mart.* 1.4–5; cf. *Pas. Perp.* 20.1.

65. Tertullian, *Apol.* 50.12–16.

66. Tertullian, *Spec.* 1.1; 30.1.

67. Merdinger, "Roman North Africa," 237. According to Tertullian, in about 190, a proconsul allowed Christians under arrest at Thysdrus to go free after reciting a statement crafted by the proconsul; the proconsul's successor, Vespronius Candidus, imprisoned a Christian for disturbing the peace but soon released him; Tertullian, *Scap.* 4.

68. Tertullian, *Mart.* 1.6.

69. Tertullian, *Mart.* 2.4.

70. Tertullian, *Paen.* 7.10; 9; 10; 12.

71. Tertullian, *Paen.* 1.21; 5.14; 9.4; 11.2–3.

72. Tertullian, *Paen.* 9.4; 11.1; *Pud.* 13.14; *Pat.* 13.2.

73. Tertullian, *Paen.* 7.10.

74. Tertullian, *Paen.* 10.8; *Pud.* 1.6; 18.18.

75. Burns, Jensen, et al., *Christianity in Roman Africa*, 299.

76. Tertullian, *Paen.* 7.2–3, 10–11; 9.1.

77. Tertullian, *Pud.* 5; 9.9; 12.5; 13.2; 19.25–28; 21.13.

78. Tertullian, *Pud.* 1.6; there was dispute over whether the bishop was from Carthage or Rome; Burns, Jensen, et al., *Christianity in Roman Africa*, 304n60.

79. Tertullian, *Pud.* 5.13–14; 7.15; 19.25–26.

80. Tertullian, *Pud.* 3.1–6.

81. Tertullian, *Pud.* 4.5; 13.12.

82. Tertullian, *Praescr.* 32.1; *Marc.* 4.5.1–2.

83. Tertullian, *Bapt.* 17; *Cast.* 7.3–6; *Praescr.* 41.8.

84. See Wilhite's discussion in which he observes that although the word *ecclesia* does not appear in the *Acts of the Scillitan Martyrs*, the text is clearly preserved for liturgical usage, and *The Passion of Perpetua and Felicity* begins and ends with the martyrs demonstrating the gifts of the Spirit given for the good of the church; Wilhite, *Ancient African Christianity*, 127.

85. Burns, Jensen, et al., *Christianity in Roman Africa*, xlviii.

86. Osborn, *Tertullian*, 35; Dunn, *Tertullian*, 32.

87. Tertullian, *Apol.* 47.4–10; *An.* 2.6–7; Dunn, *Tertullian*, 31.

88. Osborn, *Tertullian*, 10.

89. Tertullian, *Praescr.* 15.3.

90. Tertullian, *Praescr.* 19–21; 37.

91. Dunn, *Tertullian*, 21–22.

92. Dunn, *Tertullian*, 29.

93. Wilhite, *Ancient African Christianity*, 108–28.

94. Wilhite, *Ancient African Christianity*, 123–26; Dunn, *Tertullian*, 41.

95. Heffernan, *The Passion*, 304, 33n.45; Wilhite, *Ancient African Christianity*, 90.

96. Burns, Jensen, et al., *Christianity in Roman Africa*, 233.

97. Wilhite, *Ancient African Christianity*, 83. As Wilhite observes, there is no evidence of a Jewish presence in Carthage before the second century, but afterward, there can be found funeral inscriptions and even the remains of a Jewish synagogue. Only in the third and fourth centuries is there evidence of Jews and Christian sharing ritual burial sites; Wilhite, *Ancient African Christianity*, 83.

98. Merdinger, "Roman North Africa," 231.

99. Dunn, *Tertullian's* Aduersus Iudaeos: *A Rhetorical Analysis*, Patristic Monograph 19 (Washington, DC: The Catholic University of America Press, 2008), 181: "Tertullian provides us with evidence that there was both contact and conflict between Jews and Christians in

Carthage in the years of the Severan dynasty. Perhaps one could say that Christian anti-Judaic literature was written primarily for fellow Christians, but written so that they would be better prepared for ongoing encounters with Jews where the meaning of Scripture could be debated yet again."

100. Tertullian, *Apol.* 21.

101. Dunn, *Tertullian*, 47–51. As Dunn puts it, perhaps the multidimensional answer is the most fruitful; Dunn, 51.

102. Merdinger, "Roman North Africa," 234–35; for an extended treatment of Montanism, see William Tabbernee, *Prophets and Gravestones: An Imaginative History of Montanists and Other Early Christians* (Peabody: Hendrickson Publishers, 2009).

103. Dunn, *Tertullian*, 6.

104. Wilhite, *Ancient African Christianity*, 112; Gerald Bray, *Holiness and the Will of God: Perspectives on the Theology of Tertullian* (London: Marshall, Morgan, and Scott, 1979), 10–11; Tabbernee, *Prophets and Gravestones*, 94.

105. Wilhite, *Ancient African Christianity*, 113.

106. Rom. 7:14; 1 Cor. 3:1–3.

107. William Tabbernee, *Fake Prophecy and Polluted Sacraments: Ecclesiastical and Imperial Reactions to Montanism* (Leiden: Brill, 2007), 151.

108. Dunn, *Tertullian*, 9.

109. See the chart by Barnes, *Tertullian*, 55, and the discussion by Wilhite, *Ancient African Christianity*, 116–117; Merdinger, "Roman North Africa," 234.

110. Tertullian, *Scap.* 2.6.

111. Tertullian, *Nat.* 2.17.18–19; Wilhite, *Ancient African Christianity*, 118–19.

112. Tertullian, *Bapt.* 17; *Iud.* 22; *Praescr.* 3.34; 30.2; 32.1; 36.9; *Marc.* 1.21; 3.22; 4.5; *Cor.* 3.12; *Cast.* 7.19; *Ieiun.* 13.

113. Tertullian, *Bapt.* 16; *Praescr.* 36.9.

114. Tertullian, *Mart.* 1.1; CCSL 1.3: "inter carnis alimenta, benedicti martyres designati, quae uobis et domina mater ecclesia de uberibus suis et singuli fratres de opibus suis propriis in carcerem subministrant, capite aliquid et a nobis quod faciat ad spiritum quoque educandum."

115. Tertullian, *Mart.* 1.4; *Spec.* 25.14; *Cor.* 3.12; *Fug.* 3; *Pud.* 13.

116. Tertullian, *Mart.* 1.6; CCSL 1.3: "quam pacem quidam in ecclesia non habentes a martyribus in carcere exorare consueuerunt."

117. Tertullian, *Mart.* 2.6.

118. Tertullian, *Mart.* 2.5.

119. Tertullian, *Mart.* 2.7; CCSL 1.4: "immo et quae iusta sunt caro non amittit per curam ecclesiae et agapen fratrum; et insuper quae semper utilia fidei, spiritus adipiscitur."

120. Tertullian, *Mart.* 2.7.

121. Tertullian, *Iud.* 25; *Marc.* 3.7, 23; 4.9; *Mon.* 8.

122. Tertullian, *Iud.* 13.

123. Tertullian, *Or.* 2.

124. Tertullian, *Or.* 2.

125. Tertullian, *Or.* 2.

126. Tertullian, *Or.* 12.

127. Tertullian, *Bapt.* 6.

128. Tertullian, *Bapt.* 6.2; CCSL 1.282: "cum autem sub tribus et testatio fidei et sponsio salutis pigneretur necessario adicitur ecclesiae mentio, quoniam ubi tres, id est pater et filius et spiritus sanctus, ibi ecclesia quae trium corpus est."

129. Tertullian, *Bapt.* 15.

130. Tertullian, *Paen.* 10.

131. Tertullian, *Paen.* 10.6; CCSL 1.337.

132. Tertullian, *Paen.* 10.6; CCSL 1.337: "in uno et altero ecclesia est, ecclesia uero christus: ego cum te ad fratrum genua protendis christum contrectas, christum exoras; aeque illi cum super te lacrimas agunt christus patitur, christus patrem deprecatur."

133. Rankin notes that the image of the church as body is employed infrequently in Tertullian's extant writings; Rankin, *Tertullian and the Church*, 71–73; Tertullian, *Apol.* 39; *Paen.* 10; *Praescr.* 22; *Marc.* 5.19.

134. In *Against Marcion* (c. 208), Tertullian affirmed the reality of Christ's flesh while also declaring that Christ's death accomplished a spiritual reconciliation for the church. Tertullian was clear that not every mention of Christ's body in Scripture was to be taken as only a metaphor, for Christ truly possessed flesh, yet his death in the body was for the sake of the church so as to exchange a fleshly body for a spiritual one; Tertullian, *Marc.* 5.19; CSSL 1.722: "nam et supra reconciliari nos ait in corpore eius per mortem, utique in eo corpore, in quo mori potuit, per carnem mortuus et non per ecclesiam, plane propter ecclesiam corpus commutando pro corpore, carnale pro spiritali." The spiritual is no less real than the fleshly for Tertullian, and indeed, such passages indicate a priority of the spirit over the flesh. Commenting on *Marc.* 5.19, Rankin observes, "It is important to acknowledge this, for elsewhere . . . Tertullian appears to suggest both that the image bears a more concrete and less metaphorical meaning, and that there can be a real sense in which the true church (that of the Spirit) is an extension of the Incarnation and thus identifiable with the Risen Christ;" Rankin, *Tertullian and the Church*, 73.

135. Tertullian, *Pud.* 21.16; Tertullian, *On Modesty*, trans. S. Thelwall, in *The Fathers of the Third Century*, ed. A. Cleveland Coxe (ANF 4), 229.

136. Tertullian, *Pud.* 21.16; Thelwall, *On Modesty* (ANF 4), 229; CCSL 2.1328: "nam et ipsa ecclesia proprie et principaliter ipse est spiritus, in quo est trinitas unius diuinitatis, pater et filius et spiritus sanctus. illam ecclesiam congregat quam dominus in tribus posuit."

137. Tertullian, *Pud.* 2.
138. Tertullian, *Pud.* 2; 13–14; 16; 20.
139. Tertullian, *Fug.* 1.
140. Tertullian, *Mon.* 5.
141. Tertullian, *Marc.* 4.12.
142. Tertullian, *Carn. Chr.* 18.
143. Tertullian, *Res.* 8.
144. Tertullian, *Marc.* 2.4.
145. Tertullian, *Spec.* 18; 27.
146. Tertullian, *Cor.* 11.4.
147. Tertullian, *Marc.* 3.23. In this passage, Tertullian notably shifts the focus from Christ to the Holy Spirit as the agent of the building up of the church, a modification of a similar passage in *Iud.* 13.
148. Tertullian, *Marc.* 3.25.
149. Tertullian, *Bapt.* 8.
150. Tertullian, *Praescr.* 43.2.
151. Tertullian, *Iud.* 5–6.
152. Tertullian, *Iud.* 14.
153. Tertullian, *Iud.* 14.
154. Tertullian, *Iud.* 14.
155. Tertullian, *Marc.* 5.8.
156. Tertullian, *Marc.* 5.15.
157. Tertullian, *Marc.* 5.15.
158. Tertullian, *Bapt.* 9; *Pat.* 12.
159. Tertullian, *Apol.* 39; *Marc.* 4.16.
160. Tertullian, *Pat.* 12.
161. Tertullian, *Pud.* 2–4.
162. Tertullian, *Pud.* 2; 13–14; 16; 20.
163. Tertullian, *Pud.* 2; 10; *Scorp.* 5; *Marc.* 4.16.
164. Tertullian, *Pud.* 7.
165. Osborn, *Tertullian*, 181.
166. Tertullian, *Praescr.* 20.12.
167. Tertullian, *Praescr.* 20.18, 22.
168. Tertullian, *Praescr.* 20.24.
169. Tertullian, *Praescr.* 22.14; *Scorp.* 10; *Mon.* 8.
170. Tertullian, *Praescr.* 36.9.
171. Tertullian, *Scorp.* 10.

172. Tertullian, *Pud.* 28.
173. Tertullian, *Praescr.* 20.12.
174. Tertullian, *Praescr.* 21.1; 37.1.
175. Tertullian, *Praescr.* 21.2, 6; 26.15, 19, 21; 27.1, 6, 14; 36.1; 37.1.
176. Tertullian, *Praescr.* 21.2; 22.38; 28.8; 32.37.
177. Tertullian, *Praescr.* 43.1; CCSL 1.223: "ubi metus in deum, ibi grauitas honesta et diligentia attonita et cura sollicita, et adlectio explorata et communicatio deliberata et promotio emerita et subiectio religiosa et apparitio deuota et processio modesta et ecclesia unita et dei omnia."
178. Tertullian, *Praescr.* 22.38.
179. Tertullian, *Praescr.* 27.1; 37.1.
180. Tertullian, *Praescr.* 32.1, 8, 25, 37.
181. Tertullian, *Praescr.* 36.1.
182. Tertullian, *Uirg.* 2.2.
183. Tertullian, *Praescr.* 36.1, 9.
184. Tertullian, *Praescr.* 30.2.
185. Tertullian, *Praescr.* 42.1.
186. Tertullian, *Praescr.* 22.38; 28.5.
187. Tertullian makes a clear distinction between the clergy and the people using the Roman civil terminology of *ordo* and *plebs*; Hall, "The Early Idea of the Church," 51.
188. Tertullian, *Pud.* 21.17; Evans, *One and Holy*, 24, 34–35; Rankin, *Tertullian and the Church*, 29–38.
189. For an overview of the literature and arguments about the extent to which Christians and Jews interacted in North Africa, see Dunn, *Tertullian's* Aduersus Iudaeos, 16–27. Dunn concluded that the "historical and social realities of interaction between Christians and Jews were intertwined with Christian theological needs for self- definition. Thus, Tertullian could declare a parting of the ways between Christianity and Judaism on the theological level, yet still be engaged with Jews on a social basis" (Dunn, 27).
190. Tertullian, *Iud.* 2.10–14.
191. Tertullian, *Iud.* 2.10.
192. Tertullian, *Iud.* 2.12.
193. Tertullian, *Iud.* 2.10–14.
194. Osborn observed that according to Tertullian, "there are three stages in the development towards the Christian gospel: natural religion, philosophy, and Judaism;" Osborn, *Tertullian*, 45.
195. Tertullian, *Iud.* 13.24–25.
196. Tertullian, *Iud.* 14.9–10.
197. Tertullian, *Marc.* 4.16.
198. Tertullian, *Pud.* 2.
199. Tertullian, *Cast.* 2.3–5.
200. Tertullian, *Pud.* 1.8.
201. Dunn, *Tertullian*, 29.
202. Burns, Jensen, et al., *Christianity in Roman Africa*, 603.

Chapter Two

Cyprian of Carthage

Cyprian of Carthage (c. 200–258) was a significant figure in the history of North African Christianity due to his extensive writings and his original arguments for the unity of the church. Cyprian, who read the works of Tertullian and called him the "master,"[1] constructed an ecclesiology based upon unity around the bishop. According to Cyprian, apostolic succession meant that each bishop shared in the authority given by Christ to the apostles. Christ had breathed on the apostles and granted them the Spirit (John 20:22–23). The bishops, as successors of the apostles, had to maintain unity with the episcopal college in order to retain the gift of the Spirit. The power of the Spirit was only granted to those bishops who shared in the unity of the apostles by participation in the episcopal college. Thus, the bishops were granted access to the power of the Spirit by virtue of their office and their unity with one another.

Cyprian inherited the North African Christian tradition that rejected all forms of idolatry as sinful and impure. However, after listening to his brother bishops, Cyprian became convinced that the church should provide a way to reincorporate apostates and serious sinners into the one body of Christ. The members of the church must follow the proper penitential process determined by the local bishop in order to be reconciled to the community. This restoration could only be done under the supervision and authority of bishops who remained in communion with the worldwide episcopal college, as opposed to those communities that lacked apostolic authority and practiced baptism outside of the church. Cyprian argued that baptism by schismatics and heretics was not efficacious, and in this regard he was opposed to Stephen, the bishop of Rome. Before this issue was resolved, both Cyprian and Stephen died as martyrs.

Cyprian's extant works, which include 82 letters, offer detailed insight into the context, practice, and theology of the church in third century North Africa. As bishop of Carthage during a time of persecution, Cyprian had a significant impact upon the church's survival and growth in the midst of suffering. Further, his arguments for church unity helped shape Western theology and ecclesial practice, although his aim of reconciliation between Christian communities was largely unrealized at the time of his death.

THE LIFE OF CYPRIAN

The *Life of Cyprian*, composed by the deacon Pontius, was the first biography written about a Christian.[2] This *Life* did not provide any details about Cyprian's birth or early life, but Pontius claims to have been present during Cyprian's last days and death.[3] Cyprian likely was born of a wealthy family of curial class around the beginning of the third century. Scholars have posited that given his wealthy background and education, Cyprian was Romanized.[4] Prior to becoming a Christian, he received a classical education and enjoyed a successful career in Carthage as a master of rhetoric. In 246, having become disgusted with the corruption and immorality of the imperial society, Cyprian converted from polytheism to Christianity and gave his wealth to the poor. Soon after his conversion, Cyprian was ordained a presbyter, and shortly thereafter he was consecrated bishop of Carthage by the laying on of hands from Numidian bishops in 248.

After becoming a bishop, Cyprian was expected to avoid any entanglement in worldly affairs and to be committed to his ecclesiastical responsibilities. These included teaching, preaching, and celebrating the sacraments. As in Tertullian's day, the church at Carthage celebrated worship daily at the eucharistic altar as a sign of the church's unity.[5] Cyprian also emphasized Christian obligation to care for the sick and the poor. In the early 250s, a severe plague broke out in Carthage that left many dead. Cyprian instructed Christians to care for those in need, including non–Christians.[6] He also insisted that the mandate from Christ to give one's possessions to the poor extended to all Christians, not just the clergy.[7] At the same time, Cyprian frequently demanded the clergy of Carthage to release church funds to the needy. This endeared him to many in the church, yet he also found himself in the center of several controversies.

Cyprian inherited the see of Carthage during a time of societal and ecclesial discord. Within two years of Cyprian's consecration, the emperor Decius sought to unite the empire by requiring all citizens to offer sacrifices to the pagan gods.[8] All citizens were required to sacrifice to the pagan gods under the threat of torture, imprisonment, and death.[9] Decius demanded that each person sacrifice in front of witnesses in order to receive a signed certificate (*libellus*) attesting to the act of sacrifice.[10] Altars were erected in the capitol and local officials were to sign the *libellus*.[11] Anyone who did not produce a signed *libellus* was put on trial by the local magistrate. If one continued to resist, the result was imprisonment and possibly torture before a second trial before the proconsul. Many Christians died from torture and were celebrated as martyrs, while others were exiled. Some confessed their allegiance to Christ and were persecuted but not killed, and these confessors enjoyed an elevated status in the eyes of some Christians.[12] The earliest known victim of the Decian persecution was Pope Fabian in Rome in late January 250.[13]

Those Christians who renounced their allegiance to Christ were seen as guilty of committing the sin of apostasy or denying the faith. They were known as the lapsed (*lapsi*) because they had fallen from grace. This included those who had sacrificed, as well as those who had obtained the *libellus* through bribery or other means.[14] Some Christians hid among the crowds in Carthage, while others fled to distant provinces. Cyprian went into exile to an undisclosed location but kept in communication with his clergy.[15] Many criticized Cyprian for this decision, claiming that he had fled persecution, but Cyprian defended his actions and encouraged Christians to do the same in order to avoid the risk of apostasy.[16]

Decius died in battle in 251 and his order to sacrifice came to an end, bringing his sustained persecution of Christians to a close. Although brief, the Decian persecution had an immense impact upon Christianity. The church, especially the clergy, had to deal with the difficult issue of how to reconcile those who had lapsed. This required gathering bishops and calling councils in North Africa and Rome. After returning from his exile, Cyprian brought together bishops for an African council in 251.[17]

Cyprian was confronted with the challenge of how to handle apostasy in various forms. Following the tradition in North African Carthage, Cyprian decided to exclude those who had sacrificed, as well as those who had obtained a *libellus* without sacrifice, from eucharistic communion.[18] The sin of apostasy, he argued, could not be forgiven on earth since Jesus declared that he would deny before his Father those who denied him before others (Matt. 10:33).[19] Any taint of this serious sin had to be removed from the church, and none of the guilty could share in the Eucharist. Some of the lapsed sought out confessors who would claim the right to absolve them, and then produce a *libellus pacis* that declared the fallen at peace with the church. Cyprian saw this as a challenge to his authority and argued against this practice in his treatise *On the Lapsed*.[20] Those clergy who were too quick to pardon and to grant readmission to communion under the label of compassion were guilty of deceit by offering a false reconciliation.[21] Cyprian called them the laxist party, represented by the deacon Felicissimus, and their policy did not grant a share in communion but rather blocked the path to salvation.[22]

Cyprian's approach developed over time. Initially, he asserted that genuine penitents were required to spend the rest of their lives in a state of penance, and those who had received a *libellus pacis* could be restored on their death beds.[23] After listening to his fellow bishops during North African councils, Cyprian concluded that the church could provide the proper penitential process to readmit the lapsed to communion, typically after several years of penance.

The pressing issue of readmission to communion raised important questions regarding ecclesial membership. What did it mean to be in communion with the church? What constituted ecclesial unity? What authority belonged to the bishops, and what was the role of the sacraments? The answers to these questions became further complicated by the controversy that emerged in Rome, sometimes known as the rigorist controversy. After the death of bishop Fabian in 250, the local synod elected Cornelius bishop of Rome. Cornelius was known to favor leniency toward the lapsed. Novatian, a presbyter in Rome, denied the lapsed the opportunity for reconciliation with the church and found support from rigorist bishops who denounced Cornelius and chose to appoint Novatian as bishop.[24] Novatian and Cornelius sought support from other bishops, and Cyprian was faced with a difficult decision to support either a laxist or a rigorist. In the end, Cyprian decided that Cornelius had been rightly elected bishop, and that any attempt to undermine the authority of the bishops was an act of schism. To be in communion with the church meant to be in communion with the bishops. Novatian was guilty of dividing the unity of the church, and thus he was no longer in communion with the church.

The question of the sacraments came to the forefront with another controversy during Cyprian's episcopacy, this time regarding baptism. In Carthage, some Christians decided to leave the laxist party in order to join Cyprian's church. How should the church handle those who had been baptized by another party? In Cyprian's view, such Christians had not been validly baptized, and thus they need to be baptized in the true church, a position held by Tertullian.[25] The same question came up in Rome for Pope Stephen, who had been elected bishop in 254. According to Stephen, anyone who had been baptized, whether by laxists or Novatianists, was validly baptized since there was only one baptism. Such a Christian need only repent for his schism and receive the laying on of hands. The controversy between Stephen and Cyprian continued for several years through an extensive letter-writing campaign and it came to an end because of their martyrdoms under the persecution of Valerian.[26]

The persecutions under Valerian targeted Christian clergy. In August 257, Valerian issued an edict that revived persecution against those who did not follow the Roman religion. Cyprian was summoned to appear before the proconsul of Africa in Carthage. The governor read the edict, which forbade

Christians to worship and to use their cemeteries, and then exiled Cyprian to the port town of Curubis. In September 257, Cyprian had a vision in his sleep in which a youth led him to the proconsul, who immediately sentenced him to death. On this occasion, Cyprian did not go into hiding. In 258, Valerian strengthened his policy, calling for Christian clergy to be killed. Cyprian was recalled to Carthage, and on September 14, 258, his case was presented to the proconsul Galerius Maximus. After refusing to perform sacrifice to the gods, Cyprian was immediately sentenced to death by beheading. He was taken to the Ager Sexti, a large valley surrounded by trees, where he made his confession and was beheaded. According to Pontius, Cyprian was the first African bishop to be martyred, and he was remembered as the saintly bishop of the African Christian tradition.[27]

THE CHURCH IN CARTHAGE

Like Tertullian, Cyprian could claim both African and Roman identities. Although Cyprian was Romanized, he was committed to the church in North Africa and was accused of aligning with the local populace against Rome. Cyprian was also sometimes called Thascius, which some scholars have suggested might be Punic or Libyan in origin.[28] As an educated bishop whose thought was formed by principles of Roman law,[29] Cyprian's view of the church could be understood as an alternative society to that of the Roman Empire. Some scholars have maintained that Cyprian was informed by the Roman imperial ideal and assigned a religious or cosmic significance to the communion of the church in order to attain certain socio-political status, even if Cyprian remained in denial about this influence.[30] Regardless of the influence of his Roman background, Cyprian was committed to defending Christianity under the persecution of the state to the point of his own martyrdom.

Much can be gleaned about the history and practice of the church in Carthage from Cyprian's writings. Cyprian did not leave a description of the baptismal ritual in Carthage, but there are enough references in his works to reconstruct its shape. Following Tertullian, he insisted that baptism was effective only in the unity of the one church. Bishops who served in that unity guaranteed its efficacy. The rite of baptism required the invocation of the Trinity and it was followed by the giving of the Holy Spirit, normally associated with the imposition of hands upon the newly baptized.[31] The first part of the rite involved the exorcism, a rejection and casting out of demons, which was especially necessary given the work the of demons through pagan religion and entertainment. Any participation in this pagan economy, including touching altars, eating food sacrificed to the gods, or even looking at statues of Roman gods, left one stained by the contagion of idolatry.[32] Prior to the baptismal washing, the candidate made a profession of faith that involved an oath of renunciation of Satan and of idolatry in all its forms.[33] Any participation in the imperial cult would violate this oath.

Baptism required the consecration of the water in the font. According to Cyprian, the purification of the water had to be done by a bishop who had received the Holy Spirit through proper ordination in apostolic succession.[34] The bishop asked the candidates to assent to the baptismal creed, which included a question about the forgiveness of sins and the gift of eternal life through the holy church.[35] The washing with water was followed by anointing with oil, and then the imposition of hands.[36] The newly baptized were then welcomed to join the community for prayer and worship, participating for the first time in eucharistic communion. Cyprian's writings indicate that it was common in his community for infants to receive both baptism and the Eucharist.[37] While Cyprian held that infants did not have any sin of their own, nevertheless, they were born with the ancient contagion of death that came from Adam.[38]

From Cyprian's works, we see that the church in Carthage was highly organized under his episcopal leadership, with many congregations and priests under his supervision.[39] According to Cyprian, the bishop had authority in the community as a representative of Christ. The bishop offered the eucharistic sacrifice as priest,[40] and he served with judicial authority until Christ returned at the end time.[41] The bishop's office was symbolized by the commissioning of Peter as the foundation of the church.[42] The bishop regularly administered the rituals of baptism, the Eucharist, and the reconciliation of sinners, while priests and deacons could serve as his delegates.[43] Christ had founded the episcopal college upon the apostles and granted it the gift of the Holy Spirit (John 20:22–23). Only bishops who were members of that college by virtue of apostolic succession, unity in doctrine, and unity in Spirit had the power to forgive sins and to sanctify. Those who separated themselves from this episcopal unity lost the power of sanctification and with it the ability to baptize and to celebrate the Eucharist.[44] Likewise, an unworthy bishop who had committed serious sins such as apostasy no longer possessed the Holy Spirit and therefore could not perform the sacred rites.[45] This could only be applied after the bishop's sins were made known.[46] In Cyprian's view, God had allowed the persecution in order to reveal unworthy bishops through their public apostasy, and any congregation that allowed an unworthy bishop to remain shared in his sin and condemnation.[47] Other bishops who remained in communion with such a colleague were in danger of losing their own standing, and sinful bishops were to be removed from office or abandoned by their congregations.[48]

The bishop was also responsible for dispersing church funds to those in need and leading his congregation in the care of widows, orphans, and the poor.[49] Christians were obligated to offer charity toward their neighbors. By providing food, drink, and clothing to the poor, Christians helped Christ himself and would be repaid by heavenly goods.[50] Those who had failed under persecution were advised to offer almsgiving as the most appropriate means of purification and repentance leading to reconciliation and forgiveness of sins.[51]

A bishop normally served for the remainder of his life, but if he proved unworthy of his office, he could be removed by the judgment of a council.[52] Any apostate or schismatic bishops were required to submit to public penance before being allowed to enter the church among the laity, never to hold office again.[53] Cyprian left unaddressed how to handle bishops whose sins were secret and unknown. Cyprian maintained that it was sinful to support a lapsed bishop, but he did not clarify how this pertained to those who unknowingly received sacraments from a sinful bishop.[54] Although the bishop reserved the right to impose hands on the newly baptized and thus bestow the Holy Spirit,[55] presbyters and deacons could baptize when a bishop could not be present. Unlike Tertullian and Augustine, Cyprian did not make explicit mention of a provision for baptism by lay Christians in case of emergency.[56]

In Cyprian's community, the evening service continued as it did during Tertullian's lifetime, but the morning assembly became the central celebration since it included the whole community.[57] The morning service became a symbol of the unity of the church and the authority of the bishop, while schismatics violated the Eucharist by casting the flesh of Christ outside the one house and by setting up another altar.[58] In the celebration of the Eucharist, the church was united as the body of Christ, symbolized by the bread made of many grains.[59] The presider served in Christ's place to offer the eucharistic sacrifice[60] as a share in the sacrificial death of Christ and an anticipation of the heavenly banquet.[61] It also symbolized the union of Christ and the church as one body and one bride.[62] Cyprian, like other North African bishops, held that sharing in the body and blood of Christ would prepare Christians for the cup of martyrdom.[63] Unlike Tertullian, the church's holiness did not depend upon the presence of unworthy sinners in the midst of the community, although serious sinners needed to be reconciled before participating in eucharistic communion. According to Cyprian, the sacraments were holy in themselves, and those who shared in them unworthily only brought about their own condemnation.[64]

During Cyprian's time, many Christians believed that participation in the Eucharist was necessary for salvation.[65] Those who had lapsed and were excluded from communion were anxious to be received back before they died and faced judgment.[66] Some of the faithful objected, for the readmission of the lapsed would contaminate the entire communion and cut off salvation for all.[67] The holy sacrifice of Christ had to be separated from the idolatrous sacrifices of the Roman cult.[68] The idols polluted and killed, while Christ's sacrifice sanctified the worthy and harmed the unworthy.[69] Cyprian maintained that those who had lapsed had to perform the proper penance as determined by the bishop in order to be readmitted to communion. The bishop's role in determining this penitential process was underscored by the threat of renewed persecution under Emperor Gallus. In this context, the African bishops including Cyprian determined that in the case of impending imperial decree, the lapsed who had submitted to penance could return immediately to communion. The reasoning was that those who were already penitents would be strengthened and protected by the body and blood of Christ, for sharing in Christ's blood would prepare them to shed their blood for Christ.[70] Others objected that martyrdom was itself a baptism of blood that would forgive sins, therefore, reconciliation of future martyrs was unnecessary. However, the African bishops argued that penitents under the immediate threat of death would be empowered by receiving communion to confess Christ and to be strengthened for martyrdom.[71]

This demonstrated Cyprian's evolving views on the reconciliation of the lapsed and his movement away from the received tradition of Tertullian. According to Tertullian and adherents of the New Prophecy, those who committed serious sins were permanently excluded from the communion of the church. Lesser sins could be forgiven over and over through various means, including household prayer and public penance, but grave sins could not be forgiven since it was beyond the authority of the church to grant pardon. As Tertullian argued, only God could forgive sins such as adultery, apostasy, and murder. In response to the claim that Christ had conferred on Peter the keys to bind and to loosen sins, Tertullian argued that Peter received this power personally, but it was not attached to the episcopal office. Just as Peter had received powers to raise the dead and heal the sick (Acts 9:36–43; 3:1–10) but subsequent bishops had not received such powers, so too the bishops did not possess the power to forgive what only God could forgive.[72] The bishops were ministers of the sacraments, not rulers. In fact, only the truly spiritual persons held the power of forgiveness given to the church, for the authority to forgive sins came from the Paraclete.[73] Tertullian thus privileged spiritual persons, whether clergy or laity, over the bishops to grant forgiveness, precisely because the spiritual had received the Holy Spirit with certainty. The bishops did not have a unique possession of the Spirit, even if they were entrusted with carrying out the ritual of reconciliation.

Cyprian and his episcopal colleagues of North Africa offered a different understanding of the bishop's role in the forgiveness of sins and the practice of reconciliation. The African bishops adopted a policy of reconciling Christians who had confessed and repented forms of sexual irregularity classified under adultery. Individual bishops could implement new policies or retain old ones at their own discretion. Cyprian reported that this decision had no negative impact on the practice of sexual morality, continence, and virginity.[74] Most importantly, this decision demonstrated the increased authority of the bishop in the forgiveness of sins.

According to Cyprian, God forgave sins, but the bishop determined the process of penance in order to grant reconciliation with the church.[75] The penitential process consisted of acknowledgment of the sin, formal suspension from participation in the Eucharist, and admission to the status of penitent. The sinner engaged in public acts of penance, culminating in a confession of sin before the community and judgment of adequate satisfaction. The bishop and clergy then imposed hands to restore the penitent to membership and to eucharistic communion. The length of time of the process of reconciliation varied according to the kind of sin and the judgment of the bishop. In one of his later *Letters*, Cyprian determined that two years' penance was adequate for apostates who had fallen under torture during persecution.[76] Among other serious sins that required the ritual of penance and reconciliation were forms of idolatry, schism, adultery, fraud, breaking a vow of consecrated virginity, and persistent disobedience to the bishop.[77] Cyprian had come to believe that sinners bound on earth would be bound before Christ, so they had to be forgiven by the church on earth.[78] Although the bishop could not determine the interior disposition of the penitent, he could offer the opportunity to be reconciled to the church and to receive communion.

In addition, Cyprian and his colleagues, under pressure from the bishop of Rome, agreed that any penitent in danger of immediate death could be granted peace and admission to communion.[79] The practice of private reconciliation of dying penitents developed under these circumstances. A presbyter or deacon could be called to the dying person to receive the final confession, reconciliation, and the imposition of hands in order to receive eucharistic communion before death.

The consequences of apostasy differed for clergy. Presbyters and deacons were treated according to the degree of their sinfulness, and some were permitted to return to ministry. A presbyter who had sacrificed was subject to the same discipline as the laity.[80] Schismatic presbyters and deacons were allowed to return to the church but only as members of the laity.[81] Bishops who had lapsed had to be permanently removed from office. They had cut themselves off from the episcopal college, and the consequences rippled down to the rest of the congregation. The community of a lapsed bishop lacked the sanctifying power of the Spirit, thus invalidating their sacramental worship. While the church could tolerate sinners who were undergoing penance, it could not tolerate lapsed or schismatic bishops who had lost the Holy Spirit. Thus, the church was dependent upon the bishops to remain in the unity of the church.

In Cyprian's view, the church could sustain penitents who had been reconciled. The church's holiness was not dependent upon the presence of sinners, for all Christians had failures. However, the bishops were entrusted with the gift of the Holy Spirit in distinctive fashion as successors of the apostles to forgive sins. Cyprian developed his ecclesiology in order to support a change in practice in North Africa. His argument took shape in the context of the controversies he encountered during his episcopacy. Many of Cyprian's works were concerned with the nature of the church's unity, as evident in his letters and treatises such as *On the Unity of the Church*, composed while Cyprian was in hiding.[82] These works offer insight into the Biblical and theological basis for Cyprian's thought on the church. They also demonstrate how Cyprian built upon yet diverged from the renowned master Tertullian.

IMAGES OF THE CHURCH

In his treatise *On the Unity of the Church*, which some consider the first work of early Christian ecclesiology, Cyprian described the church as one yet extending into a plurality, as the rays of the sun are many but its light is one.[83] This was an allusion to the unity of the Trinity, an image that could be found in Tertullian's *Against Praxeas*.[84] Like Tertullian, Cyprian argued that the church's basis for unity was the Trinity, and in this particular passage, Cyprian identified the source of that unity as the Lord, whose light was poured forth throughout the world while remaining one.[85] Christ was the head of the church whose light was spread by the members, for while the members were many with distinct functions, they remained one body. Evoking another image from Tertullian, Cyprian spoke of the church as the one mother from whom Christians were born, nurtured, and were given life by the Spirit.[86] Cyprian made this argument in the context of his teaching on the unity of the episcopacy, with each bishop having a share in that which is one and indivisible.[87] The unity of the episcopacy was revealed in Christ's gift of the Holy Spirit to the apostles in John 20:22–23.[88] The Holy Spirit drew together the church, the one dove of Song of Songs 6:9, in the unity of the apostles, which was handed down to their successors, the bishops.[89] Just as there is one body, one spirit, and one God, so there is one church (Eph. 4:4).[90] The church was united as one body in charity because of the gift of the Holy Spirit, as mediated by the bishop. The church's unity in charity therefore was dependent upon the bishop's unity with the episcopal college.

In contrast to Tertullian, Cyprian employed such Biblical images in order to bring together the church's charismatic and institutional aspects, not to separate them.[91] That is, Cyprian resisted the tendency to set the Holy Spirit over against the visible, institutional church.[92] The church was one and holy not because of the spiritual gifts among the members, but rather because of the unity given by God to the apostles.[93] Christ built the church upon Peter (Matt. 16:18–19) so that the church's unity could be revealed by the union of the apostles around one man.[94] In *Letter* 33, Cyprian argued that the church was founded on the bishops and was governed by those who preside.[95] Each bishop had to share in the unity and authority given by Christ to Peter insofar as he remained in union with the college of bishops spread throughout the world.[96] The sanctifying presence of the Holy Spirit was guaranteed by the bishop's participation in the episcopal college, not by the purity of the spiritual members, whether clergy or laity, as Tertullian had argued.[97]

An essential feature of Cyprian's view of the church's unity was that unworthy bishops who had committed serious sins forfeited the Holy Spirit and could no longer sanctify the waters of baptism or the eucharistic offering.[98] This underscored Cyprian's emphasis upon the bishop's role in maintaining the holiness of the church. Those who had been baptized by schismatic bishops needed to be baptized within the one church because they had received false baptisms. Cyprian could apply this principle regarding the invalidation of a bishop's ministry only when serious sins were made known, as in the case of apostasy during public persecution.[99] For Cyprian, the bishop's holiness was necessary to maintain the sanctifying presence of the Spirit. The bishops provided the firm boundary around the church's unity and holiness, precisely because of their apostolic lineage and participation in the worldwide episcopal college as signified by the union of Peter with the apostles. The church was one, holy, catholic, and apostolic because of the unity of the local bishop with the universal episcopal college.

Although Cyprian held that the members of the church were imperfect, he did not take serious sins like apostasy and idolatry lightly. Like Tertullian, Cyprian emphasized the importance of not admitting the lapsed to communion immediately. Proper penance was necessary before readmission. In his writings, Cyprian reported several instances in which the lapsed attempted to partake in communion, only to be denied by miraculous events. For instance, one man became mute, while another woman bit off her tongue.[100] Children who had participated in pagan sacrifices fell into convulsions and vomiting;[101] a woman who had sacrificed to the Roman gods tried to touch the Eucharist and it burst into flames, while another man who attempted to receive unworthily found ashes in his hands.[102] These experiences informed Cyprian's views regarding the dangers of a laxist approach to ecclesial membership.

The challenges that Cyprian faced during the laxist and baptismal controversies helped shape the criteria for membership in the church. Baptism was essential in order to be a Christian. Cyprian used the image of the church as mother in order to argue that the one church alone could baptize, for "he cannot have God as his father who does not have the church as his mother."[103] Schismatics did not have valid baptism, and by separating themselves from the one family of God, they became enemies that cursed their mother.[104] Cyprian employed spousal imagery in order to speak of the one church as the bride of Christ who possessed all the legitimate power of her bridegroom and Lord.[105] This included the power to baptize, for the sacrament of baptism belonged to the one church and was a means of grace that was saving and holy.[106] The church was both mother and virgin whose fertility was abundant while remaining inviolate, chaste, and modest.[107] Heretics and schismatics could not baptize with the church's baptism because they were working against the church,[108] and they remained outside of the ark.[109] Those who were baptized became a temple of God, but if one denied Christ or God the Father, the Holy Spirit could not dwell in him.[110] The Holy Spirit worked through the visible, institutional church, which dispensed the grace of God through the sacraments. These sacraments were efficacious because of the bishop's unity with the episcopal college. If a bishop had cut himself off by schism or any other serious sin, his baptism was no longer efficacious, and his congregation could not receive the sanctifying waters or the true communion of the Lord's body and blood.

NO SALVATION OUTSIDE OF THE CHURCH

According to Cyprian, baptism in the one church was necessary for salvation, yet Cyprian followed the tradition of baptism by blood for those who confessed Christ and died as martyrs.[111] Cyprian was clear that heretics should not be granted the title of martyrs because of their false confession of Christ. In this context, Cyprian famously declared that since there is no salvation outside of the church (*salus extra ecclesiam non est*),[112] the washing of water by heretical sects had no effects, and consequently those who came to the church from a heretical group needed to receive the one true baptism of the holy church.[113] In Cyprian's theology, to say that there is no salvation outside of the church meant that baptism belonged to the one church that alone had the power to dispense grace and to sanctify because of the gift of the Spirit given by Christ to the apostles and their successors.

Cyprian found himself at odds with Pope Stephen on the issue of the validity of baptism practiced by schismatic groups. Cyprian claimed an African tradition of the need to baptize heretics, while Stephen held a tradition in which those who had been baptized in heresy could receive a rite of the imposition of hands without repeating their baptism.[114] Stephen made this argument based upon a distinction between the imparting of the Holy Spirit and baptism in the name of Jesus,[115] but Cyprian declared that the Holy Spirit was received through baptism.[116] The church, as the one bride of Christ (*solam sponsam christi*), alone could conceive and give birth to children of God through the Holy Spirit.[117] Stephen's position would prevail following Augustine's development of it, but Cyprian offered a coherent view of the efficacy of baptism based upon the work of the Holy Spirit through the sacraments celebrated by the church. Only those who have the Holy Spirit can grant baptism, forgive sins, and offer the Eucharist.[118] The presence and activity of the Spirit depended upon the bishop's unity with the episcopal college. The ministers who celebrated sacraments on the bishop's behalf had to be empowered by a bishop who possessed the Holy Spirit. Thus, Cyprian privileged episcopal unity over the spiritual gifts of lower clergy or laity, for only the bishops could mediate the unity shared by Peter and the apostles. One could not give what one did not have. The bishops had to be in unity with the episcopal college in order to have the Spirit and to remain in the unity of the church.

The Eucharist was central to Cyprian's view of salvation. The Eucharist offered a share in the sacrifice of Christ and anticipated the heavenly communion of the church. The Eucharist was a foretaste of the eternal life enjoyed by the saints and angels in heaven. Cyprian permitted changes in the practice of reconciling sinners in order to offer penitents the hope of true salvation. The church's unity, as received in communion, had an eschatological aim insofar as it anticipated a final eschatological communion.[119] Unlike Tertullian, Cyprian did not collapse the eschatological *ecclesia* with the historical church on journey, for while there was an eschatological urgency in expectation of an imminent end,[120] the church was pure and holy as the one spouse of Christ,[121] awaiting final judgment. The Lord allowed the church to undergo testing, including the rise of heresies, so that pure faith might be revealed even before the day of judgment, as the chaff was divided from the wheat.[122] Penitents did not threaten the church's purity or holiness. However, lapsed and schismatics bishops were sources of disunity and spiritual death. The church was one and holy because the bishops maintained their unity and holiness by sharing in the episcopal college. There was no salvation outside of the church empowered to share in the sacraments because of the power to sanctify given by the Christ and the Spirit to the apostles and their successors, the bishops.

CONCLUSION

While Cyprian came to reject a kind of rigorism that denied any readmission to the sacraments in favor of a more moderate penitential approach influenced by his episcopal colleagues in North Africa, Cyprian nonetheless maintained strong boundaries around the church based upon the local bishop. Only the bishop could determine the proper penance for those who had lapsed, and the bishop was responsible for the local congregation's unity with the church due to his unity with the episcopal college. This meant that congregations were always under the threat of separation from the church because of the local bishop's sins or doctrinal errors. Thus, while Cyprian certainly mitigated the rigorism of Tertullian, according to which those guilty of serious sins were expelled permanently in order to keep the church pure and holy, Cyprian maintained a strict view of church membership based upon unity with the bishops. If a local bishop forfeited unity by serious sin or by erroneous teaching, the local community was cut off from the church's invisible union in charity. This could create serious problems, especially because the sins of the bishop could be hidden from the congregation. What would happen to the local church if the bishop was secretly a heretic, schismatic, or adulterer? Christianity in the fifth century continued to grapple with these issues, and Augustine and others sought to provide different ways of understanding the basis for the church's unity in the Spirit in order to overcome some of the difficulties associated with Cyprian's theology.

Like Tertullian before him, Cyprian understood the church as distinct from and opposed to the "world" (*saeculum*).[123] The bishop exercised a unique kind of spiritual and judicial authority, as handed on by the apostles. The church was a universal society constituted by the law of God and governed by the bishops in order to preserve the peace and concord of Christ. It was the bishop's duty to preserve the unity and peace of the church. Charity was a mark of the episcopacy, and the church's bond of charity was maintained by episcopal unity. To be a Christian, it was necessary to be in union with a bishop who was joined to the worldwide episcopal college. While upholding Cyprian's legacy as saintly martyr who pursued unity, Augustine departed from Cyprian's theology by offering a rich and distinctive understanding of the efficacy of the sacraments, the church's mediation of charity, and the Spirit's work to bring about salvation through the one church.

NOTES

1. Wilhite, *North African Christianity*, 114.
2. Burns, Jensen, et al., *Christianity in Roman Africa*, 32.
3. Pontius's *The Life of Cyprian* can be found in CSEL 3.
4. Wilhite, *North African Christianity*, 142, 147–54; Allen Brent, *Cyprian and Roman Carthage* (New York: Cambridge University Press, 2010); J. Patout Burns, *Cyprian the Bishop* (London: Routledge, 2002).
5. Henry Chadwick, *The Church in Ancient Society: From Galilee to Gregory the Great* (New York: Oxford University Press, 2001), 148.
6. Cyprian, *Mort.* 14.
7. Cyprian, *Eleem.* 7.
8. Burns, Jensen, et al., *Christianity in Roman Africa*, 12–15.
9. Cyprian, *Ep.* 40.1.1.
10. Cyprian's letters seem to indicate that virtually all inhabitants, regardless of status, sex, and age were required to perform the sacrificial rites; Cyprian, *Ep.* 15.4; 55.13.2; *Laps.* 9; 25.
11. Cyprian, *Ep.* 43.3.1; *Laps.* 8; 25.
12. Wilhite, *North African Christianity*, 143; Rebillard, *Christians*, 53.
13. Burns, Jensen, et al., *Christianity in Roman Africa*, 15n79, 12n66.
14. Cyprian, *Laps.* 27–28; *Ep.* 15.3.1; 20.2.2, 55.14.1. The practice of bribing one's way out of persecution was common in earlier North Africa, as testified by Tertullian, although Tertullian disapproved of it; Tertullian, *Fug.* 5.3, 12–14; Burns, Jensen, et al., *Christianity in Roman Africa*, 17.
15. Cyprian, *Ep.* 20.

16. Cyprian, *Ep.* 7; 8; 20.

17. The result of this council led Cyprian to change his mind, moving away from his severe approach described in his work *On the Lapsed* to a moderate view detailed in *Letter* 55; Burns, Jensen, et al., *Christianity in Roman Africa*, 28; see especially Cyprian, *Ep.* 55.3.2–7.3.

18. Hall, "The Early Idea of the Church," 52.

19. Cyprian, *Laps.* 20.

20. Cyprian, *Laps.* 14; 17–20.

21. Cyprian, *Laps.* 15.

22. Cyprian, *Laps.* 16; on the formation of this party, see Geoffrey D. Dunn, *Cyprian and the Bishops of Rome: Questions of Papal Primacy in the Early Church* (Strathfield, NSW: St Pauls, 2017), 30, and "Heresy and Schism According to Cyprian of Carthage," *Journal of Theological Studies* 55: 2 (2004), 551–74.

23. Cyprian, *Ep.* 20.2.1–2.

24. Wilhite, *North African Christianity*, 145; James Papandrea, *The Trinitarian Theology of Novatian of Rome: A Study in Third-Century Orthodoxy* (Lewiston: Edwin Mellen Press, 2008).

25. Tertullian, *Bapt.* 15.2.

26. Cyprian, *Ep.* 67–75; Wilhite, *North African Christianity*, 145; J. Jayakiran Sebastian, *"baptisma unum in ecclesia sancta": A Theological Appraisal of the Baptismal Controversy in the Work and Writings of Cyprian of Carthage* (Hamburg: Lottbeck Jensen, 1997).

27. Wilhite, *North African Christianity*, 146.

28. Wilhite, *North African Christianity*, 150–51.

29. Brent, *Cyprian and Roman Carthage*, 24.

30. Brent, *Cyprian and Roman Carthage*, 37; Burns, *Cyprian the Bishop*, 46–47.

31. Cyprian, *Ep.* 69.12.1–14.2.

32. Cyprian, *Laps.* 15–16; 23–26; *Ep.* 31.6.2–3.

33. Cyprian, *Laps.* 8; *Ep.* 13.5.3; Tertullian, *Spec.* 4.24.

34. Cyprian, *Ep.* 70.3.1; *Sent.* 18.

35. Cyprian, *Ep.* 69.7.1–2; 70.2.1; 73.4.2.

36. Cyprian, *Ep.* 73.6.2; 69.11.3; 72.1.2; 74.5.1.

37. Cyprian, *Laps.* 25.

38. Cyprian, *Ep.* 64.5.2.

39. Wilhite, *North African Christianity*, 146; Burns, Jensen, et al., *Christianity in Roman Africa*, 6, 370–81.

40. Cyprian, *Ep.* 63.14.4.

41. Cyprian, *Ep.* 59.5.1; 66.4.2.

42. Cyprian, *Ep.* 43.5.2; 46.1.2.

43. Cyprian, *Ep.* 16.2.3; 63.14.1; 76.3.1.

44. Cyprian, *Ep.* 70.

45. Cyprian, *Ep.* 65.2.2, 4.1; 66.5.1.2; 70.

46. Cyprian did not make provision for dealing with the secret and unknown sins of a bishop and the efficacy of his ministry; see Burns, Jensen, et al., *Christianity in Roman Africa*, 181.

47. Cyprian, *Ep.* 65.3.1–3; 67.3.1–2.

48. Cyprian, *Ep.* 67.5.4, 9.1–3; 65.4.2; 68.

49. Cyprian, *Ep.* 7.1.

50. Cyprian, *Eleem.* 24; *Mort.* 26; *Hab. uirg.* 11.

51. Cyprian, *Laps.* 35; *Unit. eccl.* 26; *Ep.* 55.22.1, 28.1.

52. Burns, Jensen, et al., *Christianity in Roman Africa*, 377.

53. Cyprian, *Ep.* 64.1.1; 67.6.3; 72.2.1–3.

54. Burns, Jensen, et al., *Christianity in Roman Africa*, 181.

55. Cyprian, *Ep.* 73.9.2.

56. Cyprian, *Ep.* 18.1.2, 2.2.

57. Cyprian, *Ep.* 63.2.1, 15.

58. Cyprian, *Unit. eccl.* 9; 17.

59. Cyprian, *Ep.* 63.13.4.

60. Cyprian, *Ep.* 57.14.4.

61. Cyprian, *Ep.* 63.9.2–3.
62. Cyprian, *Ep.* 63.13.1–3.
63. Cyprian, *Ep.* 57.2.2, 3.2; 58.1.2.
64. Cyprian, *Laps.* 25–26.
65. Cyprian, *Ep.* 55.17.2; 57.4.1–4.
66. Cyprian, *Ep.* 55.29.2; 57.1.1.
67. Cyprian, *Ep.* 55.28.1–29.2.
68. Cyprian, *Ep.* 55.11.2–3; 65.2.1–3.3; 67.1.1–3.2.
69. Cyprian, *Ep.* 57.2.2; 24; *Laps.* 15–16; 23–26.
70. Cyprian, *Ep.* 57.2.2; 58.1.2.
71. Cyprian, *Ep.* 57.4.1–2.
72. Tertullian, *Pud.* 21.1–7.
73. Tertullian, *Pud.* 21.17.
74. Cyprian, *Ep.* 55.20.2, 21.1.
75. Cyprian, *Ep.* 55.20.3.
76. Cyprian, *Ep.* 56.2.1.
77. Cyprian, *Ep.* 3.4; 43.1.2; 41.2.1; 50.1.2; 55.21.2; 67.5.3; 69.7.1.
78. Cyprian, *Ep.* 57.1.1, 3.3, 4.3–5.2.
79. Cyprian, *Ep.* 55.13.1.
80. Cyprian, *Ep.* 64.1.1.
81. Cyprian, *Ep.* 72.2.1–3.
82. Cyprian's *Unit. eccl.* was written in two stages, with Cyprian editing the work in a later controversy; Burns, Jensen, et al., *Christianity in Roman Africa*, 186n120.
83. Cyprian, *Unit. eccl.* 5; CCSL 3.253: "ecclesia una est quae in multitudinem latius incremento fecunditatis extenditur: quomodo solis multi radii sed lumen unum, et rami arboris multi sed robur unum tenaci radice fundatum, et cum de fonte uno riui plurimi defluunt, numerositas licet diffusa uideatur exundantis copiae largitate, unitas tamen seruatur in origine. auelle radium solis a corpore, diuisionem lucis unitas non capit; ab arbore frange ramum, fractus germinare non poterit; a fonte praecide riuum, praecisus arescit."
84. Tertulian, *Prax.* 8.5–7; Evans, *One and Holy*, 53–55.
85. Cyprian, *Unit. eccl.* 6; CCSL 3.254: "dicit dominus: 'ego et pater unum sumus', et iterum de patre et filio et spiritu sancto scriptum est: et tres unum sunt. et quisquam credit hanc unitatem de diuina firmitate uenientem, sacramentis caelestibus cohaerentem, scindi in ecclesia posse et uoluntatum conlidentium diuortio separari? hanc unitatem qui non tenet non tenet dei legem, non tenet patris et filii fidem, uitam non tenet et salute."
86. Cyprian, *Unit. eccl.* 5; CCSL 3.253: "sic et ecclesia, domini luce perfusa, per orbem totum radios suos porrigit, unum tamen lumen est quod ubique diffunditur nec unitas corporis separatur; ramos suos in uniuersam terram copia ubertatis extendit; profluentes largiter riuos latius spandit, unum tamen caput est et origo una, et una mater fecunditatis successibus copiosa: illius fetu nascimur, illius lacte nutrimur, spiritu eius animamur."
87. Cyprian, *Unit. eccl.* 5.
88. Cyprian, *Unit. eccl.* 4.
89. Cyprian, *Unit. eccl.* 4; CCSL 3.252: "quam unam ecclesiam etiam in cantico canticorum spiritus sanctus ex persona domini designat, et dicit: 'una est columba mea perfecta mea, una est matri suae, electa genetrici suae'."
90. Cyprian, *Unit. eccl.* 4; CCSL 3.252: "unum corpus et unus spiritus, una spes uocationis uestrae, unus dominus, una fides, unum baptisma, unus deus?"
91. "In what we may interpret as an explicit rejection of Tertullian's views, he located sanctifying power and authority to govern in the office of bishop rather than allowing it to be shared among all the members. He explained that Christ had conferred these powers on the bishops, initially represented by the apostles, and not on Peter alone. The gifts were conferred on the elected leader of each local church through his induction into the episcopal college through the ritual of consecration by his counterparts in other churches. This theory of the transmission of the power of the Holy Spirit from Christ through the apostles into the episcopal college and thence into the local church by its leader's membership in the college was a coherent and scripturally based explanation which justified the structures of governance within

the community, the efficacy of its sacramental rituals, and the binding force of decisions reached by individual bishops and synods. In theory and practice, it withstood the challenge mounted by the laxist and rigorists who survived the Decian persecution. The differentiation of the clerical role and the rejection of Tertullian's egalitarian views enabled a greater cohesion and stability within the local community"; J. Patout Burns, "Establishing Unity in Diversity," *Perspectives in Religious Studies* 32:4 (2005): 387–88.

92. Michael Sage says that Cyprian saw organization and episcopal power as "the most essential ingredients for salvation," and thus the efficacy of sacraments is tied fundamentally to an institution, which binds the power of the Holy Spirit; Michael Sage, *Cyprian* (Cambridge, MA: The Philadelphia Patristic Foundation, 1975), 248.

93. Vasilije Vranic has shown that for Cyprian, unity is divinely given, in contrast to the later Donatists, for whom holiness is logically prior to ecclesial unity; Vasilije Vranic, "Augustine and the Donatist Claims to Cyprianic Ecclesiological Legacy," *Philotheos* 7 (2007): 208–221; Cyprian, *Unit. eccl.* 8.7–8.

94. Cyprian, *Unit. eccl.* 4.

95. Cyprian, *Ep.* 33.1.1.

96. Cyprian, *Unit. eccl.* 4–7; *Ep.* 33.1.1–2; Burns, Jensen, et al., *Christianity in Roman Africa*, 327.

97. Burns, "Establishing Unity in Diversity," 388.

98. Cyprian, *Ep.* 65.2.2, 4.1; 66.5.1–2.

99. Burns, Jensen, et al., *Christianity in Roman Africa*, 378.

100. Cyprian, *Laps.* 24.

101. Cyprian, *Laps.* 25–26.

102. Cyprian, *Laps.* 26.

103. Cyprian, *Unit. eccl.* 6; *On the Church: Select Treatises*, trans. Allen Brent (Crestwood: St. Vladimir's Seminary Press, 2006), 157; CCSL 3.253: "habere iam non potest deum patrem qui ecclesiam non habet matrem;" *Ep.* 74.7.1–2.

104. Cyprian, *Ep.* 73.19.2.

105. Cyprian, *Ep.* 73.11.1.

106. Cyprian, *Ep.* 73.11.2.

107. Cyprian, *Unit. eccl.* 5–6; 19.3; *Laps.* 2.

108. Cyprian, *Ep.* 73.11.2.

109. Cyprian, *Unit. eccl.* 6; CCSL 3.253: "si potuit euadere quisque extra arcam noe fuit, et qui extra ecclesiam foris fuerit euadet."

110. Cyprian, *Ep.* 73.12.2.

111. Cyprian, *Ep.* 73.21.1; Tertullian, *Bapt.* 16.1; *Paen.* 13.7.

112. Cyprian, *Ep.* 73.21.2; CCSL 3C.555.

113. Cyprian, *Ep.* 73.21.3; CCSL 3C.555–56: "et ideo baptizari eos oportet qui de haeresi ad ecclesiam ueniunt, ut qui legitimo et uero atque unico sanctae ecclesiae baptismo ad regnum dei regeneratione diuina praeparantur sacramento utroque nascantur, quia scriptum est: nisi quis natus fuerit ex aqua et spiritu, non potest introire in regnum dei;" *Ep.* 72.1.3.

114. Burns, *Cyprian the Bishop*, 118–31.

115. Cyprian, *Ep.* 74.5.1.

116. Cyprian, *Ep.* 74.7.1; CCSL 3C.571–72: "porro autem non per manus inpositionem quis nascitur quando accipit spiritum sanctum, sed in baptismo, ut spiritum iam natus accipiat, sicut in primo homine adam factum est. ante eum deus plasmauit, tunc insufflauit in faciem eius flatum uitae."

117. Cyprian, *Ep.* 74.7.2; CCSL 3C.572: "nec enim potest accipi spiritus, nisi prius fuerit qui accipiat. cum autem natiuitas christianorum in baptismo sit, baptismi autem generatio et sanctificatio apud solam sponsam christi sit, quae parere spiritaliter et generare filios deo possit, ubi et ex qua et cui natus est qui filius ecclesiae non est?"

118. Cyprian, *Ep.* 69.11.1; 73.7.1; 74.4.2.

119. The church's bonds of unity are not just terrestrial, but eschatological; see J.A. Gil-Tamayo, *Cyprian: Obras completas* (Madrid: BAC, 2013).

120. Cyprian retains an eschatological urgency in the midst of persecution; see the discussion by Evans, *One and Holy*, 59.

121. Cyprian, *Unit. eccl.* 6; CCSL 3.253: "adulterari non potest sponsa christi, incorrupta est et pudica: unam domum nouit, unius cubiculi sanctitatem casto pudore custodit."

122. Cyprian, *Unit. eccl.* 10; CCSL 3.256–57: "sic probantur fideles, sic perfidi deteguntur, sic et ante iudicii diem hic quoque iam iustorum adque iniustorum animae diuiduntur, et a frumento paleae separantur. hic sunt qui se ultro aput temerarios conuenas sine diuina dispositione praeficiunt, qui se praepositos sine ulla ordinationis lege constituunt, qui nemine episcopatum dante episcopi sibi nomen adsumunt; quos designat in psalmis spiritus sanctus: sedentes in pestilentiae cathedra: pestes et lues fidei, serpentes ore fallentes et corrumpendae ueritatis artifices, uenena letalia linguis pestiferis euomentes; quorum sermo ut cancer serpit, quorum tractatus pectoribus et cordibus singulorum mortale uirus infundit."

123. Cyprian, *Demet.* 18–19.

Chapter Three

Augustine of Hippo

Augustine of Hippo (c. 354–430) was a pivotal figure in the development of Latin ecclesiology. Augustine attempted to carry forward the traditions from Tertullian and Cyprian while providing new ways of understanding sacramental efficacy, ecclesial membership, and the church's mediation of salvation. Augustine's originality can be seen in his multivalent view of the church as visible and invisible, historical and transcendent. His thick and sophisticated theology of the church established definite boundaries and defined criteria for ecclesial membership. However, it was not always apparent if such criteria were met, for the Holy Spirit worked invisibly, and the believer's interior disposition remained hidden. As Augustine famously declared, there were some who seemed to be within the church but were not, while there were others who seemed to be outside but were within.[1] In order to understand what this meant for Augustine, it is necessary to examine the growth of his thought in the midst of theological disputes over the course of his life, particularly with the Donatists in North Africa. It is also important to understand the changing status of Christianity as a religion in relation to the empire during Augustine's time.

CHRISTIANITY IN AUGUSTINE'S TIME

Christianity in the fourth and fifth centuries experienced seismic changes during the shift from being a persecuted religion to becoming the predominant religion of the empire. This transition was sparked by the Edict of Milan and Constantine's support of Christianity in the early fourth century, and it reached a high point with the decree of Theodosius in 379 that recognized Catholic Christianity, as confessed by the bishops of Rome and Alexandria, as the official form of Christianity in the empire.[2] Augustine lived during a time that saw the rise and fall of Rome to the Visigoths, and eventually the invasion of North Africa by the Vandals. The precariousness of politics led Augustine to exhort his congregation to place their hopes in the heavenly city of God rather than in any earthly kingdom or empire.

In North Africa, the changing political dynamics came into play with the emergence of a Christian schism that would later require imperial intervention. The Donatist controversy, as it would be known, developed as a result of the persecution of Diocletian in the early fourth century.[3] Diocletian issued a series of edicts that required sacrifice and targeted Christian clergy, demanding them to "hand over" (*traditor*) the Scriptures and sacred items to be destroyed. Any clergy who did so were called *traditores*, and they were deemed guilty of apostasy and the contagion of idolatry by the faithful. Many Christians rejected the ministry of those who had lapsed during persecution. After the death of the bishop of Carthage around 312 and the subsequent election of Caecilian, some of the faithful refused to accept this election because of the accusation that one of the consecrators had handed over the Scriptures to the imperial authorities. Whether or not this accusation was true, Caecilian and his supporters were known to follow the practice of the Roman church of refusing to rebaptize those who had entered their communion after having been baptized by *traditores*, schismatics, or heretics. This was distinct from the third-century African practice defended by Cyprian, whose disagreement with Pope Stephen was never resolved. Yet both Caecilian and his opponents claimed to be heirs to Cyprian. Those who opposed Caecilian elected Majorinus as bishop, and after his death shortly thereafter, they elected Donatus. The Donatists worshipped separately, and they maintained churches across Africa, southern Spain, and even one in Rome.[4] Caecilian was vindicated by commissions of bishops at Rome in 312 and Arles in 314, and Caecilian's group, which was supported by emperors and bishops outside of Africa, became known as Catholics.

From 317 to 321, Constantine attempted to bring the Donatists into union with the Catholics using imperial forces, which resulted in the deaths of a number of people, including a Donatist bishop in Carthage. However, in 321 Constantine gave up on these attempts at coerced unity in order to focus on political matters. Donatism continued to grow during the rest of the fourth century, such that by Augustine's time, Donatists formed the majority of Christians in some parts of North Africa.

Scholars have shown that Donatists and Catholics were difficult to distinguish in practice and faith.[5] The point of contention had to do with whether or not Caecilian had been contaminated by idols through the laying on of hands by a *traditor*. In fact, at the beginning of the controversy, both parties would have agreed that such contamination invalidated ordination; the supporters of Caecilian simply claimed that it did not happen. Augustine would provide the argument that any such contamination would not invalidate ordination, just as the baptism performed by *traditores*, schismatics, and heretics was not invalidated by the ministers.[6] Thus, Augustine is responsible for developing a coherent theology of sacramental validity based upon the Roman tradition while remaining, in his own estimation, faithful to the tradition of Cyprian and North Africa.[7] To what extent Augustine was faithful to Cyprian's theology is a matter of debate.[8]

Regardless of the degree to which Augustine carried forward the African tradition, it is clear that he offered an original vision of the church shaped by the context in which he lived and wrote. A brief summary of his life will enable us to see how Augustine formed his singular and influential contribution to Latin ecclesiology.

AUGUSTINE'S LIFE

Augustine was born on November 13, 354, in Thagaste, modern day Souk Ahras Algeria. Augustine's mother, Monica, was a practicing Catholic, and his father, Patricius, was a pagan who converted to Christianity at the end of his life. As a child, Augustine was brought to the church to be initiated but baptism was withheld, as it was commonly practiced. Despite his mother's devout faith, Augustine spent his youth outside of the church in search of various forms of community, friendship, and pleasure.[9] At the age of nineteen, he studied rhetoric at Carthage, and there he took a concubine who bore him a son, Adeodatus. Augustine also studied the works of Aristotle and Cicero, and he eventually became attracted to the Manichean religion. Mani, the founder of the sect, claimed to possess a special revelation of light, and his followers identified him as the Paraclete. The Manicheans posited a strict separation between good and evil, light and darkness, spirit and matter. Good and evil were two eternal powers constantly at war, and the material world was the consequence of the struggle between light and darkness. The elect, who were aware of this constant battle, practiced extreme kinds of fasting in order to release the light that had become mired in material bodies. The Manichean myths were attractive to Augustine because they helped explain the tension between good and evil in every person.[10] However, after meeting the incompetent Manichean bishop Faustus, Augustine became disillusioned with the religion because of its inadequate answers to his questions, especially about the nature of good and evil.[11]

During the 380s, Augustine taught rhetoric in Thagaste, Carthage, and Rome before taking up a position as professor of rhetoric in Milan. There he encountered important imperial officials, many of whom had become Christians. He also met the Catholic bishop of Milan, Ambrose, who showed Augustine how to interpret Scripture while utilizing philosophy, particularly the works of Neoplatonists such as Plotinus and Porphyry. From the Neoplatonists, Augustine understood that God is being and goodness itself, and that evil is no thing. From Ambrose, Augustine learned how to uncover the mysteries hidden in the Scriptures after having previously considered the Bible too simplistic and unsophisticated. Augustine found Christianity not only intellectually and socially credible, he also found it theologically convincing and morally transformative.

Augustine came to understand that the church was the medium of salvation, precisely by means of the sacraments. In book 8 of *Confessions*, Augustine recounted several conversion stories, noting the necessity to make the profession of faith in the church by being baptized, as in the case of African Marius Victorinus.[12] In spite of the struggles from his former way of life, Augustine was baptized on April 25, 387, and he gave himself over to prayer, study, and contemplation. Returning to North Africa, he intended to form a monastic community but soon found himself forced into ministry. While attending worship in Hippo Regius in 391, Augustine was seized by the crowd and forcibly ordained to serve the Caecilianist bishop Valerius. As a priest and pastor, Augustine immediately faced controversy. The Donatists opposed his ordination and claimed that he was still a Manichean. After being elevated to the episcopacy in 395, Augustine was opposed by a Numidian bishop because of an accusation that Augustine had used a love potion on a certain woman.[13] Augustine wrote extensively against the Manichaens and the Donatists during this time. He also became engaged in disputes with Pelagius, Julian of Eclanum, and pagan *literati*. In the year 410, the sack of Rome by Alaric and the Visigoths prompted Augustine to write his lengthy *City of God*, a work that deconstructed the mythology of the Roman pantheon while constructing a positive theology of the church and Christian worship.

Near the end of his life, while continuing to write against the Donatists and Pelagians, Augustine witnessed the siege of North Africa by the Vandals. He died on August 28, 430, and less than one year later, the city of Hippo fell to Vandal invaders. These events and controversies helped shape Augustine's thought on the church, which developed from his earlier, more philosophical writings to his later mature works. As he continued to study the Scriptures, especially the letters of Paul in the 390s, Augustine's Biblical theology became the key to his ecclesiology.[14] To be sure, the influence of philosophy, especially the Neoplatonism of Plotinus, remained in Augustine's mature writings. It was used in order to help clarify the central doctrines of faith revealed in the Scriptures and in the Christian tradition. However, the Christian teachings were mysteries that could not be reduced to any philosophical system. Further, it is important to remember that Augustine was a bishop while he wrote most of his theological works, and his ecclesiology can be found not only in his writings but also in his preaching. His mature thought on the meaning of the church developed in the context of his life as a pastor in North Africa.

THE CHURCH IN ROMAN NORTH AFRICA

Augustine's many writings and sermons provide access to the life and practices of the Latin church in the fourth and fifth centuries. Like his predecessors Tertullian and Cyprian, Augustine understood the Christian life as marked by participation in the sacred rites of the church, charity toward one's neighbor, and the pursuit of ecclesial unity in the hope of eternal salvation. In Augustine's time, church membership was a lifelong process of transformation, purification, and growth in holiness in order to be saved.

By the fifth century, Christian parents often enrolled their children as catechumens shortly after they were born, but many delayed baptism, as in the case of Augustine. Children in danger of death were granted emergency baptisms. Catechumens were signed with the cross and received the imposition of hands and a taste of salt.[15] There was no clear minimum length of the catechumenate for adult converts, and many who were dedicated as infants lived as catechumenates for most of their lives. They regularly attended sermons, especially from the bishop, but were not allowed to be present for the eucharistic prayer and communion. Baptism could be celebrated at any time, but Easter was the most appropriate time. At the beginning of the Lenten preparation each year, catechumens would be invited to submit their names for baptism. Those who responded were called *competentes*, or co-petitioners, and they began the process for full reception into the community, which included fasting, almsgiving, and instruction. The *competentes* received baptism during the Saturday Easter vigil service. They were required to reject Satan and to swear allegiance to Christ. After being asked creedal questions to prompt the confession of faith, they were baptized by the bishop with the washing of water (either submersion or pouring over the head) and the use of the Triune formula. The neophyte was then clothed in white linen, symbolizing purity and new birth, before being anointed with oil and receiving the imposition of hands calling down the Holy Spirit. Augustine followed Tertullian in his understanding of the anointing as conferring a share in Christ's universal priesthood.[16] The newly baptized were then welcomed to join the community for prayer and eucharistic communion. The neophytes returned for instruction and wore their baptismal robes for the following week while participating in daily eucharistic communion.

In Augustine's context, the normal minister of baptism was the bishop or a cleric he had authorized. The bishop alone was permitted to bless the oil used in the anointing since it signified the sending of the Holy Spirit given to the apostles and handed on by apostolic succession. Augustine argued that the ritual of baptism could be performed by anyone, even an unbeliever, as long was the proper form was used,[17] although this was not common. Schismatic and heretical baptisms were valid, as long as the proper Trinitarian formula was declared. As part of this argument, Augustine distinguished between the sacramental reality effected and the sanctification communicated. That is, anyone who received baptism properly was marked and claimed for Christ permanently, similar to a military tattoo. The sanctification that followed came from the Holy Spirit's gift of charity to love God and neighbor, yet this could be lost immediately if one rejected the faith. In Augustine's view, the exterior administration of the sacrament was efficacious, but the interior disposition also played an important role. It was possible to reject the gift of charity by serious sin. However, charity could be restored at any time by the imposition of hands in the sacrament of reconciliation.[18]

As we shall see, Augustine argued that Christ himself gave baptism through the minister, but the church was the mediator of sanctification because the Holy Spirit conferred the power to forgive sins upon the whole church. In continuity with Tertullian rather Cyprian, Augustine argued that in Matthew 18:18, the power to bind and to loosen was given to the whole church. The church's unity of charity was found in the invisible communion of charity among the whole Christ, head and members. Augustine turned to 1 Peter 4:8 to argue that charity covered a multitude of sins, and that the Spirit's gift of charity enabled the church to forgive sins. The power to forgive sins, which was mediated by the sacraments such as baptism and reconciliation, found its source in unity of the whole Christ. The minister of baptism acted as the agent of Christ and of all the saints as his ecclesial body united in charity. Thus, the church's power to sanctify did not depend upon the bishop's union with the episcopal college, instead, this power belonged to all of the faithful, although the bishop administered the sacraments and gave the imposition of hands. According to Augustine, unity in charity meant the ability to love God and neighbor and to forgive one another's sins.

One key aspect of Augustine's teaching was that although baptism could be found outside of the visible church, it belonged to the Catholic Church, and it would confer salvation only to those who intentionally sought union with the saints.[19] As a result, in an emergency, Catholic catechumens could receive baptism from a Donatist cleric, and they would gain the salvific effects by their intention to join the loving unity shared by Catholic saints, not the false unity of schismatic rebels.[20]

The Eucharist was a special sacrament. Like baptism, the efficacy of the sacrament originated from Christ rather than the minister. Therefore, when celebrated by a validly ordained minister, the bread and wine were transformed into the body and blood of Christ, independent of the holiness of the minister.[21] However, the reality (*res*) of the Eucharist was more than just the flesh and blood of Christ. According to Augustine, the reality of the eucharistic communion included the unity of the whole Christ, head and members, as one body in charity.[22] Schismatics could not receive this reality since they had, by definition, cut themselves off from the unity of the church. Thus, schismatics could celebrate the Eucharist, but they did not receive the fullness of the reality it signified nor the sanctification it conferred.

Following the tradition, Augustine recognized serious sins that required exclusion from the Eucharist. These demanded confession in public or private, the performance of penitential works, and formal release from guilt. Among these major sins were murder, adultery, fornication, theft and robbery, false witness, as well as the list provided by Paul in Galatians 5:19–21, including sorcery, enmity, jealousy, anger, dissension, party spirit, envy, and drunkenness.[23] Since idolatry was no longer the same challenge to Christians in a Christianized empire, Augustine focused on idolatry through astrology, spells, and incantations.[24] Augustine also identified the sexual abuse of slaves as the most common form of adultery.[25] In the category of minor sins of daily living were the immoderate use of bodily necessities, failures in social life, and lapses of attention in prayer. The sins of daily living could be forgiven by forgiving others, by private and communal recitation of the Lord's prayer, and by almsgiving and fasting. Some of the faithful abstained from the Eucharist, while others insisted eucharistic communion was a necessary medicine for purification from minor sins. Augustine honored both practices.[26]

Departing from the North African tradition represented by Tertullian, Augustine argued that all sins could be forgiven by means of the ritual of reconciliation.[27] Charity covered a multitude of sins, both major and minor. Serious sins required formal public penance as determined by the bishop, and those sinners who did not repent had to be excommunicated.[28] The length of penance was established by the bishop according to the particular sin.[29] The bishop could also assign private penance in order to protect Christian sinners who were guilty of crimes that could be punished through imperial courts.[30] Clergy who were guilty of serious sins were removed from office and communicated among the laity,[31] although exceptions were made for Donatist clergy, who might be allowed to retain their office for the sake of unity.[32]

As in his teaching on baptism, Augustine distinguished between the authority and action of the bishop administering penance and the forgiveness of sins offered by the whole church. The clergy were the ministers of reconciliation, but the power to forgive sins was received from the Holy Spirit as the gift of charity possessed among the society of saints, that is, all those united in love.[33] Like baptism, the sacrament was efficacious through the ritual, but the interior disposition of the penitent was also significant, for the penitent had to have the intention of union with the saints.[34] Following Tertullian, Augustine argued that the Holy Spirit was the source of the unity and holiness of the church, and the Spirit's gift of charity united the members as one body. Unlike Tertullian, Augustine held that this communion of charity could and did forgive serious sins due to the divine power given to the saints.[35] The only unforgivable sin against the Holy Spirit was a rejection of the church's unity and a failure to seek the forgiveness of the saints.[36] The consequence of Augustine's view was that the bishops did not determine the efficacy of the sacrament themselves, even though they were the normal ministers of reconciliation. The Holy Spirit belonged to all of the saints, not merely to the bishops in union with one another. Further, Augustine's theology meant that the society of saints could forgive those who were truly penitent, even if they had not received the ritual. This did not obviate the need for the sacrament, instead, it demonstrated the power of the Holy Spirit to work beyond visible limits, and to bring salvation to a penitent who might have died without the opportunity to receive the ritual.[37] Augustine's sacramental theology did not relegate the power to sanctify exclusively to the bishops, as Cyprian's had, yet it still accounted for the normal mediation of grace by means of the church's administration of the sacraments.

Augustine rejected Cyprian's understanding of the bishop's exclusive power to sanctify, but he accepted the role of the bishops in governing the church. The source of this governing authority was not the unity of the episcopal college derived from the unity of Peter and the apostles; rather, the bishop's power to forgive came from the whole body of Christ, head and members. Christ was the one mediator between God and humanity, but that included all of the members who shared in Christ's priesthood. Christ was the one priest, and the ministers were priests precisely as members of the whole body.[38] Augustine also acknowledged the need for apostolic succession of the bishops.[39] As a rightful successor of the apostles by the proper lineage of ordination, the bishop exercised his role by ordaining clergy and governing them. The bishops worked together in councils in order to make important ecclesial decisions, and only bishops could suspend or remove an unworthy bishop.[40] However, the bishops found their governing authority from the whole Christ.[41] The church's unity depended not upon the local bishop, but upon the charity of the Holy Spirit, which had been poured upon the hearts of the faithful (Rom. 5:5). The Holy Spirit operated by means of the visible church's sacraments in order to grant the gift of charity, but the Spirit was not limited by visible things. Thus, although a bishop might be in visible schism, the members of his congregation could remain in the unity of the church by intending to join the unity of charity mediated by the Catholic Church. Participation in charity and the Holy Spirit did not depend upon the bishop's moral status or unity with the episcopal college. However, those who wished to be united to the saints in charity should seek to receive the sacraments of the Catholic Church in order to enter into full communion.

The main lines of Augustine's mature ecclesiology emerged in his writings against the Donatists and in his sermons. In what follows, I will focus primarily upon these works, although other writings will be addressed as necessary in order to grasp Augustine's complex thought on the church. Augustine offered a renewed exegesis of Biblical images of the church in his understanding of the church as one, holy, Catholic, and apostolic.

IMAGES OF THE CHURCH

One of the predominant images of the church in Augustine's works was the body of Christ. He spoke of the church as Christ's body for the first time in his treatise *On Genesis Against the Manichees* (c. 388/389), in which Adam and Eve in Genesis 2:24 were figures of Christ and the church.[42] Just as the two became one flesh, so Christ and the church were one body (Eph. 5:31–32), with Christ as the head.[43] The creation of Eve from Adam's side prefigured the formation of the church as Christ's spouse (*conjux*) from his side as he slept on the cross.[44] The church was born from the side of Christ, that is, by the sacrament of baptism, signified by the blood and water that poured out from Christ's side.[45] The sacraments gave birth to new members of the one body, particularly baptism, the sacrament of regeneration[46] by which new members could be incorporated into the body of Christ.[47]

Baptism was essential for Augustine because it built up the church as one body united in charity. In the prologue of *Teaching Christianity* (begun c. 396 and completed in 420), Augustine drew attention to the fact that Paul received divine instruction from heaven, yet he was sent to receive the sacraments in order to be joined to the church.[48] Even the solitary monk Antony, who knew the divine Scriptures by heart, was raised in a community. Augustine emphasized the need for community so that people might be bound together by the knot of unity, which is charity.[49] In book 1, Augustine declared that the divine wisdom became flesh in order to forgive sins and to bind the members of his body with the "knot of unity and love."[50] The church was the society united in the love of God and neighbor,[51] and each member was "conceived by the Holy Spirit" through baptism.[52] By means of the "holy bath," the faithful gave birth to the twin fruit of charity, that is, the love of God and neighbor.[53] The church in essence was a social body, united in the bond of charity.

The church was one and holy because of charity, precisely as a gift of the Holy Spirit. Augustine's view of charity was based upon his reading of Scripture, especially the writings of Paul, in the 390s. Charity moved a Christian to love God and neighbor for God's sake, to perform good works as commanded by Christ, and to forgive offenses so as to receive forgiveness.[54] However, Augustine maintained that charity was imperfect among the fallen members of the church on pilgrimage.[55] This applied to both clergy and laity. All Christians were fallen, and all were sinners. Yet some become saints by the grace of God. The perfect union of the saints in charity could not be harmed by the presence of the imperfect undergoing transformation by the grace of the sacraments. The church's unity in charity could bear with the presence of the wicked, for charity covers a multitude of sins.

Drawing upon the dissident Donatist theologian Tyconius, Augustine held that the visible church was a mixed body of good and wicked, wheat and chaff.[56] The weeds were found among the wheat (Matt. 13:24–30), and they would not be separated until the end. In the meantime, God permitted this intermingling during the church's historical pilgrimage on earth. Augustine used the figure of Noah's ark in order to illustrate the church's mixed condition. "All the kinds of animals are enclosed in the ark, like all the nations.... Both clean and unclean animals are present there, just as both good and bad people are found together in the sacraments of the church."[57] This interpretation was in direct contrast to Tertullian, who employed Noah's ark to convey the church as free from the impurity of idolatry.[58] Whereas Tertullian used the figure of the ark to construct an exclusivist, perfectionist ecclesiology,[59] Augustine showed how the church on earth, that is, the Catholic Church, included good and wicked, elect and reprobate. Baptism was necessary for entrance into the one church, the body of Christ, built up in history by means of the sacraments just as the ark was completed to attain its full measure.[60] The Holy Spirit worked in order to bind together the members of the church in the unity of love, and this love was able to endure any kind of scandal or sin.

In his anti-Manichean work *Against Faustus* (c. 399), Augustine began to construct an ecclesiology based upon a rich pneumatology. The church's unity was constituted by charity as a gift of the Holy Spirit, which provided a framework of unity that could withstand any kind of scandal, whether from within or without.

> The timbers of the ark are glued together with pitch on the inside and on the outside in order to signify the tolerance of love in the framework of unity, so that fraternal unity does not yield to the scandals that try the church, whether from those who are inside or from those who are outside, and so that the bond of peace is not destroyed. For pitch is a very hot and strong glue that signifies the ardor of love, which tolerates all things with great strength in order to maintain a spiritual community.[61]

The church is bound by charity, the love of God poured out on our hearts by the Holy Spirit (Rom. 5:5), one of Augustine's favorite verses.[62] There were seven pairs of clean animals in the ark to symbolize the sevenfold gifts of the Holy Spirit at work among the good who "preserve the unity of the Spirit in the bond of peace" (Eph. 4:3).[63] Augustine associated the Holy Spirit with charity, such that the Spirit could be spoken of as the love that unites the members, just as the Spirit unites the Father and the Son.[64] The church's unity originated in the Trinity, particularly in the Holy Spirit as the love that unites Father and Son as one. Augustine moved back and forth between saying that the Spirit constituted the church as one and that charity constituted the church as one.[65] Regardless, it is clear that charity and the Holy Spirit were inseparable. Drawing upon Optatus, Augustine argued that charity could tolerate and forgive sins,[66] and this charity could only be found in the Catholic Church, which has the Spirit.[67] Charity was mediated by baptism, precisely through the visible anointing that brought about the invisible anointing in the Holy Spirit, that is, the anointing of charity.[68] In Augustine's thought, to receive and abide in the Holy Spirit meant to possess charity as a divine gift.[69]

Augustine used the figure of Noah's ark to show that the church is one, yet it exists in several conditions: 1) as the elect, chosen by God before the creation of the world; 2) on pilgrimage in history as a mixed body of good and wicked; and 3) in eschatological perfection. The figure of Noah's ark was polyvalent, for it conveyed multiple aspects of the one church. In Genesis, God created the world in six days, and Augustine understood the "days" to mean the six ages of God's works in history, beginning with the age from Adam to Noah.[70] The ark was constructed out of four-sided beams, just as the church was built out of the holy ones ready for every good work (2 Tim. 2:21), that is, the elect.[71] The ark contained both clean and unclean animals, signifying the good and the wicked found in the sacraments of the Catholic Church.[72] In this sense, the ark represented the church in its mixed condition, which "now floats on the waves of the world, and is saved by the wood of Christ's cross."[73] However, the ark could also point to the eschaton, when all of the members will be brought into final unity. For just as the dove was sent out and brought back the branch of an olive, so some who were baptized outside of the church and did not lack charity might be brought "to the unity of communion by the mouth of the dove, as if by the kiss of peace."[74] The dove was sent out after seven days and did not return again.

> This signifies the end of the world, when the rest of the saints will no longer be found in the sacrament of hope, by which the church is united in the present time, when we drink what flowed from Christ's side, but will already be in the perfection of eternal salvation, when the kingdom will be handed over to him who is God the Father, so that in that clear contemplation of immutable truth we shall not need bodily sacraments.[75]

In this passage from *Against Faustus*, Augustine has begun to work out a way in which those who were baptized outside of the church might be brought into communion with the one church by charity. This does not mean that such charitable ones form a separate body from those holy ones inside the visible church. There is only one body of Christ, one body of charity, to which all the saints are joined. This is the very body built up by means of the sacraments of the Catholic Church. The good, who are properly the body of Christ, must bear with the wicked and tolerate sinners in order to grow in patience and to avoid abandoning those who might become good.[76] To abandon Christ's body is to abandon Christ. Those who remain outside of the church and do not have charity, such as the Donatists, will be destroyed by the flood.[77] However, those who are separated from the church but do not seek their own glory but the glory of Christ will not perish from the flood, and these are the charitable ones who will be joined to the one church at some future time.[78]

As we shall see, Augustine continued to develop this line of thought in his writings against the Donatists, but the seeds of his ecclesiology had already been planted in his works from the 390s. Augustine engaged other Biblical images of the church in order to distinguish between the mixed church in history and the eschatological church in perfection. The church was the spotless bride of Christ, without stain or wrinkle (Eph. 5:27) in glory,[79] yet she had to undergo a process of growth and transformation in order to be purified from sin.[80] The true spouse of Christ is the Catholic Church, not any other group that preaches a different gospel.[81] She was the one chaste spouse and virgin mother because of her teaching from Christ,[82] however, she was also filled with sinners guilty of adultery. The church was the temple of God, the holy church composed of true and genuine Christians,[83] but during this time, the church of Christ is the one that rises up and is seen by all, that is, the Catholic Church,[84] filled with the holy and unholy.

As the body of Christ, the church is on pilgrimage in this world,[85] until the saints are finally taken up from the "mourning of its pilgrimage into the glory of everlasting salvation."[86] As members of Christ's body, the church forms the whole Christ. For while Christ the head is above in heaven, he is below on earth in his body, the church.[87] Christ became flesh so that we might become the body of the head.[88] There is only one Christ, and there is only one church united in charity. This charity is preserved in the good members, who properly form the body of Christ,[89] but during this time, the church is a mixed body. Precisely in this condition, the "ardor of love" can tolerate all things, including the presence of sinners, in order to maintain a "spiritual community."[90]

In his figural exegesis of Scripture, Augustine distinguished between the visible church celebrating the sacraments and the invisible communion of saints united in charity. This was a distinction without separation, for the church is one and holy. Against the Donatists, Augustine argued that the church's holiness did not depend upon the minister, for the church was holy because of the presence of Christ and the Spirit. Likewise, the sacraments were efficacious not because of the moral status of the minister, but because of the power of Christ. In this argument, Augustine rejected Cyprian's idea of the church's unity around the episcopal college as the guarantee of the

Spirit's power. Instead, the Spirit worked through the sacraments regardless of the minister. Even schismatics had baptism, and thus they did not need to be rebaptized. However, those who received the sacraments while in schism cut themselves off from the effects. Cyprian was to be venerated because he prized unity over division, but he wrongly attached the power to sanctify to the episcopal college. Augustine's teaching on apostolic succession shared some similarity with Tertullian's, for Augustine recognized the need for apostolic lineage for the laying on of hands and the preservation of true doctrine. However, Augustine rejected Tertullian's rigorism and exclusivist ecclesiology, for the invisible communion of saints had the power to forgive serious sins and to welcome back the penitent into the one communion of charity.

AGAINST THE DONATISTS

Around the year 400, Augustine began a series of works addressing the issues raised by the Donatist controversy. This provided him with the opportunity to flesh out many of the arguments he had begun in the 390s. In his *Answer to the Writings of Petilian*,[91] Augustine addressed the issue of rebaptism by arguing that Christ, not the minister, was the source and origin of regeneration and the head of the church.[92] Whether one received the sacrament of baptism from a faithful or an unfaithful minister, it was Christ who justified the ungodly (Rom. 4:5).[93] Christ baptized in the power of the Holy Spirit (John 1:33).[94] Christ sanctified, cleansed, and purified his bride, the church.[95] Baptism was efficacious because it belonged to God, not to the minister.[96] Augustine followed the North African bishop Optatus of Milevis in the claim that the efficacy of the church's ministry depended upon divine power.[97] Sinful ministers did not diminish the power of the sacraments.

Further, Augustine argued that the presence of sinners among the community celebrating the sacraments did not destroy the holiness and purity of the church. Citing John 15:3, in which Christ told the apostles "you are already made clean," Augustine declared that the uncleanness of some cannot hurt those who are clean.[98] The bad do not hurt the good, just as the chaff does not hurt the grain, and both are found in the church until the Lord comes to clear the threshing floor and to burn the chaff in unquenchable fire (Matt. 3:12).[99] The saints are the grain, in whom charity and holiness reside by the power of the Spirit.[100] This charity could not be harmed, for no matter how many sinners were found among the sacraments, the one church could not be divided.[101] Augustine thus rejected a rigorist approach that denied the reconciliation of sinners because of an erroneous understanding of charity.

Along these lines, in *Answer to the Letter of Parmenian* (c. 400), Augustine asserted that the church does not cease to exist because of the presence of sinners. In this matter, Augustine claimed to follow Cyprian, who upheld ecclesial unity over a kind of purity based upon a sinless church.[102] Cyprian therefore could not be claimed by the Donatists, nor did he fall into the same kind of rigorism advocated by Tertullian. However, Augustine argued against Cyprian's practice of rebaptizing schismatics. In Cyprian's view, this was not rebaptism but true baptism since schismatics did not possess the power to sanctify. Augustine claimed that baptism existed outside of the church and had effects because of Christ who baptizes and confers the Holy Spirit. The unworthy minister who performed the sacrament outside of Catholic unity did so at his own peril.[103] Once conferred, baptism could not be lost once just as a royal stamp or military tatoo were not lost, even if used illegally. "Inasmuch as we see that apostates, upon whom it is certainly not conferred again when they return through penitence and therefore cannot be judged to have lost it, do not lack baptism, is it possible that the Christian sacraments adhere less strongly than this bodily tatoo?"[104] Likewise, ordination could not be lost among schismatics, for "just as baptism in them has remained integral, so has their ordination, because in their schism there had been a defect that was corrected by the peace of unity; [that defect] was not in the sacraments."[105] Those who were ordained properly and within the apostolic lineage still possessed the right to confer ordination, as they did for baptism, yet if they did so without the unity of charity, it was to their own destruction.[106]

In *On Baptism* (c. 400/401), Augustine accused the Donatists of lacking charity despite having the sacraments.[107] Although Cyprian did not perceive the hidden depth of the sacraments, he did have charity and remained in the unity of the church. In his humility and willingness to be corrected, Cyprian followed the example of Peter.[108] Peter served as a model for the whole church, not merely the bishops or the episcopal college. Like Cyprian, Augustine held that there was only one church, which was called Catholic, and one baptism.[109] This baptism belonged to Christ, and it was holy of itself.[110] Baptism even forgave the sins of those in heresy or schism, but because of their dissent, their sins returned immediately and they were cut off from the unity, charity, and peace of the church.[111] They possessed true baptism, but it was the church's baptism. She gave birth to everyone through baptism, even those outside of the visible Catholic Church.[112] The church was the one mother who bore children by means of Christ's baptism.[113] Those who were separated from the unity of the church could not beget children, for there was only one mother.[114]

Drawing upon figures from the Old Testament, Augustine declared that Donatists who were born by baptism could arrive at the promised land if they came to the unity of peace found in the church. If not, they would come to belong to the portion of Ishmael rather than Isaac, Esau rather than Jacob.[115] The church gave birth to spiritual (*spiritalis*) persons, but all were born in

Adam first as carnal (*carnalis*) or animal (*animalis*; 1 Cor. 15:46, 1 Cor. 2:14).[116] The church, the people of God and an ancient reality on pilgrimage, has an animal portion in some but a spiritual one in others.[117] The new covenant pertains to the spiritual and was hidden in the old, but when the Lord came in the flesh, the new was revealed.[118] There were certain spiritual persons who lived under the sacraments of the old covenant,[119] just as there were some who live in a fleshly or animal way under the new sacraments. The spiritual persons were born of the church, including Abel, Enoch, Noah, Abraham, Moses, and the prophets, just as the church gave birth to the apostles, martyrs, and all good Christians.[120] Augustine suggested that all of the holy ones before Christ and after have been born by the church, and the sacrament of baptism had effects for those of the old covenant.[121] The power of baptism extended beyond the visible limits, even beyond the limits of time. For the sacraments of the old covenant provided a mysterious participation in the future sacraments instituted by Christ, which were greater in power but fewer in number.[122] All of the just beginning with Abel were spiritual persons, born from the womb of the church. Thus no one was to be despaired of, whether the carnal who were found in the church or the adversarial who were found outside, for God will separate the chaff at the end time. Spiritual persons however, including the just before Christ, are not outside because they are rooted by the immense power of charity upon the rock of unity.[123]

For Augustine, the Spirit worked to mediate charity through the visible church's rituals, but the Spirit could not be limited by them. Following the North African tradition before him, Augustine affirmed that the martyrs received baptism by blood, yet if charity was lacking, then martyrdom was of no benefit.[124] The martyrs were joined to the very charity mediated by the baptism of the Catholic Church. The Holy Spirit was given only in the Catholic Church by the laying on of hands, as Cyprian declared,[125] yet Augustine understood this to mean that all who were cut off from communion with the Catholic Church lacked charity, for "he who does not love the church's unity does not have God's charity, and for that reason it is rightly understood to be said that the Holy Spirit is not received except in the Catholic Church."[126] The Catholic Church was the medium of salvation because of the mediation of the Holy Spirit, yet the Spirit could bring some outside of the church into the union of charity. Those who were brought in, however, had to share in the love of Catholic unity possessed by the one church. That is, they had to seek the unity in charity enjoyed by the saints and angels in heaven, and by the holy ones on pilgrimage. In the context of *On Baptism*, Augustine referred specifically to those who possessed valid baptism outside of the Catholic Church as the ones who could be joined to the church by sharing in the charity given by the Spirit. Thus, baptism remained necessary for salvation, for the Donatists had valid baptism, and even the

Jews had some kind of participation in baptism by virtue of their sacraments or rituals such as the works of the law. These examples attest to Augustine's confidence in the power of the Spirit to mediate charity by means of the sacrament of baptism, even if baptism did not take the normal form of ritual washing and the imposition of hands. For martyrs were baptized in blood, the righteous of the Old Testament were born of mother church, and schismatics could be brought to the communion of the one church at some future time due to the charity mediated by baptism, which belonged to the Catholic Church.

In effect, Augustine expanded the boundaries of the church by arguing that while there is one visible Catholic Church, the invisible communion of charity extended beyond visible bounds. This did not obviate the visible community, nor did it render the sacraments meaningless or ineffective. For although there were some who had not received the cleansing with water through the ritual of the church's baptism, nevertheless, all of the spiritual were born from the womb of the church. If charity could be found outside of the visible church, baptism would not be lessened or rendered unnecessary. Rather, one could argue that in Augustine's theology, the sacrament of baptism does more rather than less, precisely because it has effects beyond the visible church. The visible church remains essential because of the celebration of sacraments such as baptism, and as a sign of the unity shared among the members of the one body, a unity effected by the sacraments.

In his understanding of the unique role of the bishop of Rome as successor of Peter, Augustine interpreted Peter served as a visible sign of the unity of the whole Christ, head and members. The power given to Peter in Matthew 16:19 was a symbol of the unity of the one perfect dove (Song of Sol. 6:8).[127] The dove refers to the spiritual saints in the church.[128] Christ's gift of the Holy Spirit to the apostles in John 20:22–23 was a gift to the entire church, for the apostles represented the person of the church,[129] and Peter was a sign of the church's unity as the one rock.[130] Apostolic succession was necessary, as found in earlier theologians such as Tertullian and Cyprian, but it served as a safeguard of unity with the whole church, represented by Peter. "For if the order of the succession of bishops is to be considered, with how much more certainty and indeed benefit do we count back from Peter himself, to whom, as bearing in a figure the whole church, the Lord said, 'Upon this rock will I build my church, and the gates of hell shall not prevail against it.' Linus succeeded Peter, Clement succeeded Linus. . . . In this order of succession, no Donatist bishop is found."[131] Augustine thus used apostolic succession in his argument against the Donatists, yet it was based upon an understanding of Peter as a sign of the union of the whole church. The church's peace resides only in the good, "whether those who are already spiritual or those who by their peaceful obedience are making progress toward spiritual things. It is not in the bad, though, whether they are acting troublesomely outside [the church] or are being endured with groaning within, both baptizing and being baptized."[132] The invisible bond of peace excluded the wicked within the visible church, establishing firm boundaries within that were known to God alone.[133] For God knows whom he has predestined before the foundation of the world (Rom. 8:29) to be conformed to the Son, and there are many outside of the church who might be joined to the one dove and the bride of Christ without stain or wrinkle.[134]

Predestination formed part of Augustine's doctrine of the church in the anti-Donatist writings. In book 5 of *On Baptism*, Augustine referred to the church as the bride of Christ without stain or wrinkle in order to indicate the number of the predestined.[135] The beautiful dove is the lily, the enclosed garden and a sealed fountain (Song of Sol. 2:2, 4:12) in those righteous persons who constitute "the set number of saints that was predestined before the creation of the world."[136] The number of the righteous will be revealed on the last day, but until then, the good and the wicked are mixed together in the church, such that "many who seem to be outside are within, and many who seem to be within are outside."[137] This is only possible because of charity since to be in the church, according to Augustine, means to have charity as a gift of the Holy Spirit without which there is no salvation.[138]

Augustine developed an ecclesiology that could be described as both inclusivist and exclusivist. The church included sinners who had repented and performed penance, as well as all of the just before Christ, and all who were united to the church in charity while being outside of the visible communion. The church excluded those inside the communion who did not have charity and cut themselves off from the effects of the sacraments due to sin. The church's boundaries were firm, but they were not discernible to the naked eye. In Augustine's view, the invisible bond of charity defined ecclesial membership, but God alone knew those whom he had predestined for salvation.

On a pastoral level, uncertainty about one's status in the church need not lead to despair, rather, it could be cause for hope. For while the interior disposition of the believer had to remain open to charity, in Augustine's teaching, charity was a gift freely offered to the faithful by means of the sacraments. The sacraments were efficacious and holy no matter what the condition of the minister or recipient.[139] If one committed serious sins and cut oneself off from the church, one could receive forgiveness of sins by the prayers of the saints,[140] as mediated by the sacrament of reconciliation. The prayers of the saints had effects for those outside of the visible church as well. Augustine agreed with Cyprian that outside of the church, no one could bind or loosen and nothing could be bound or loosened,[141] but those who were at peace with the dove were loosened even if they were outside, while those who were not at peace were bound, whether inside or outside.[142] At the end time, the bride without stain or wrinkle would be revealed. In the meantime, the church on pilgrimage remained a mixed body while on journey toward the final separation of wheat from chaff.[143] This mixed condition provided the opportunity for the wicked to be converted and the good to grow in forbearance and love. One need not seek to be perfectly free from the stain of sin, as in Tertullian's context, nor would one have to rely upon the bishop's holiness in order to be sanctified. Instead, according to Augustine's ecclesiology, one could receive the gift of charity from the Holy Spirit by means of the sacraments while trusting in the slow but steady process of purification and sanctification afforded by the church's liturgical and communal life.

The pastoral implications of Augustine's thought on the church are evident in his sermons, which provide access to his mature ecclesiology in the context of pastoral ministry in North Africa. These sermons are theologically rich since they gave Augustine the opportunity to explore the mysteries of Scripture and to interpret Biblical passages at length. In his preaching, Augustine offered a coherent ecclesiology based upon a sophisticated Christology and pneumatology.

THE CHURCH IN AUGUSTINE'S PREACHING

Augustine's incarnational Christology is the foundation for his ecclesiology in his sermons. Christ, the Word of God, became flesh in the womb of the virgin Mary so as to become the head of the church. All of the members are joined to that flesh in order to become one body.[144] The whole Christ (*totus Christus*) is Christ the head and the members "in the fullness of the church."[145] In the Scriptures, Christ could be identified in three ways: 1) as God according to the divine nature and coequal with the Father; 2) as God incarnate, having assumed flesh and become human while remaining God, the only mediator between God and humanity;[146] and 3) as the whole Christ, head and members, united as one body.[147] The whole Christ was "predestined before time began, when there was neither morning nor evening."[148] God's plan prior to creation was to become incarnate in order to unite Christ the head and his body, the church.

In his exegesis of the Psalms, Augustine claimed that the words of the Psalmists could be spoken by either Christ the head or the members of his body.[149] Christ speaks in the members of his body whether they are at rest or in labor,[150] and though Christ was sinless, he prayed the penitential psalms in his sinful members.[151] The members of the body can speak as one with the head because of the bond of charity.[152]

> Without him, we are nothing, but in him we too are Christ. Why? Because the whole Christ consists of head and body. The head is he who is the savior of his body, he who has already ascended into heaven; but the body is the church,

toiling on earth. Were it not for the body's linkage with its head through the bond of charity, so close a link that head and body speak as one, he could not have rebuked a certain persecutor from heaven with the question, Saul, Saul, why are you persecuting me? (Acts 9:4).[153]

The distinction between head and members was not lost, yet the members of the body could speak with Christ in one voice.[154] This union between the head and the members in charity allowed Augustine to develop an ecclesiology of solidarity, wherein Christ the head shares in the sufferings of the members of his body on pilgrimage. "He is the head, we are the body. Accordingly, when we hear his voice, we must hearken to it as coming from both head and body; for whatever he suffered, we too suffered in him, and whatever we suffer, he too suffers in us."[155] Christ suffers in his members, although the head does not suffer in heaven.[156] Christ takes on the sufferings of the members on pilgrimage while offering them salvation.[157] By the virtues of faith, hope, and charity, the members of the body already begin to share in heaven with the head.

> Our head, Christ, is already in heaven, but our enemies can still rage against us.... He said that he was here below in us; therefore we are also there above in him, because even now he has raised my head above my enemies. Look how wonderful a pledge we have, assuring us that we too are in heaven for ever with our head, in faith and hope and love, because our head is with us on earth in divinity, in goodness, in unity, even to the consummation of this age.[158]

In the midst of suffering, the members of the body are being transfigured into the head so as to be further conformed to Christ in faith, hope, and charity.[159] Augustine preached on the meaning of suffering to his congregation in order to encourage the members of the church to find their identity as members of the whole Christ while undergoing suffering.

The members of Christ's body include not only those who come after Christ in history, but also those holy ones who came before him, as evident in the examples of the holy men and women of the Old Testament.[160] As in his work *On Baptism*, Augustine made the unique claim that the body of Christ included all of the just from Abel to the end of the world.[161] All of the righteous since the world began have Christ as their head.[162] Some of the members of Christ's body have preceded the head in time, nevertheless, all are united as one body because of Christ's sacrifice on the cross.[163] Abel is a just man who prefigured Christ by his martyrdom out of his love for God and by an act of true sacrifice.[164] The church continues on pilgrimage in history from Abel until the end of time.[165]

One of Augustine's favorite images for the church in his preaching is city. The church is the heavenly city of God on pilgrimage in this world. There are two cities formed by two loves, Jerusalem by the love of God and Babylon by the love of the world.[166] The citizens of the cities are intermingled during the present age,[167] but the citizens of the wicked city of Babylon can become members of the city of Jerusalem by receiving baptism.[168] Yet the members of Jerusalem may return to Babylon by returning to sin.[169] The citizens of Jerusalem must bear with the citizens of Babylon, who are in the church and sometimes are in charge of affairs that concern Jerusalem.[170] The good must bear with the wicked in the church with love in order to be conformed to the patience and forbearance of God that leads to repentance,[171] until the winnowing takes place and the grain and straw are separated so that the faithful drawn from the human race are joined with the heavenly angels to form the one house and one city of God.[172]

The city of God is the body of Christ, whose head is its king.[173] The soul of the one body of Christ is the Holy Spirit, for just as the soul unites the different members of a body, so the Holy Spirit unites the members of the church.[174] The Holy Spirit's gift of charity unites the church as one body and one fellowship. This charity is operative in the rituals of baptism, Eucharist, and reconciliation. In particular, the Eucharist signifies and makes present the unity of the one body as a present reality, in anticipation of the final eschatological union.

> Thus by this food and drink he wishes that the fellowship of his body and of his members be grasped; that fellowship is the holy church in his saints and his faithful, who have been predestined, and called, and justified, and glorified; of these stages the first has already happened, that is, predestination; the second and third both have happened and are happening, that is, calling and justification; while the fourth, that is, glorification, is now only to be had in hope, to be realized in the future. The sacrament of this reality, that is, of the unity of Christ's body and blood, is placed on the Lord's table and received from the Lord's table—in some places every day, in others at fixed intervals of time, leading some to life and others to ruin. But, the reality itself, of which this is the sacrament, means life for all, ruin for none, no matter who shares it.[175]

The Eucharist offers life to those who possess charity, but destruction to those who participate in it unworthily. Yet the unity of the body could not be harmed, no matter who shared in it. According to Augustine, charity was stronger than sin. Augustine emphasized the need for participation in the visible body celebrating the sacraments in order to grow in charity.

The life of the community in Jerusalem as described in Acts 2:43–47 offered a model of the Christian community in anticipation of the heavenly life of the blessed.[176] Augustine encouraged the ideal of shared possession in clerical communities, as well as a sharing of income and goods among the local congregation.[177] By loving and supporting the members of the body, Christians were serving Christ in one another.[178] Augustine did not limit almsgiving to members of the city of God, for Christians should be generous to pagans, Jews, and heretics.[179] While the citizens of the cities were intermingled, Christians should demonstrate charity to all with the hope that others would come to share in the heavenly city by the grace of God. Augustine continued to explore the meaning of Christian worship and the grace mediated by the sacraments in later works such as *City of God* and his writings against the Pelagians.

AGAINST THE PELAGIANS AND THE PAGANS

In his classic work *City of God* (c. 413–427), Augustine offered a deconstruction of the pagan system of worship along with a construction of the true worship of the Christian church.[180] God's providence was responsible for the rise and fall of kingdoms in the world, but human beings remained active agents in the midst of history. The lust for glory and the pride of the Romans led to their downfall. The Christian church did not shoulder the blame for Rome's fall, for the Romans brought about their own destruction. According to Augustine, the purpose of true religion was not to build worldly kingdoms, but to cling to the truth, that is, to cling to God and thereby to find true happiness. The true worship of the Christian church built up the city of God, not any earthly city. At the daily eucharistic worship of Christians, the whole church was united as one fellowship and one city, the one body of Christ, head and members. The whole Christ consisted of the head in heaven and all the saints and angels, as well as all of the members of the body on pilgrimage on earth, united in charity.[181] The church offered this sacrifice as a sign of the final eschatological unity, and as a means of deepening charity among the members of the body.

Human beings were created in order to share in the fellowship of charity. This was revealed in the creation of Eve from Adam's side. "God chose to create [Adam] as one for the propagation of a multitude precisely for the purpose of admonishing us that we should maintain unity (*unitas*) and concord even when we are many. And the fact that the woman was made for him from his own side also signifies just how precious the union between husband and wife should be."[182] Adam and Eve prefigured the unity of Christ and the church, a unity accomplished through the sacraments "by which the church is built up" (*quibus aedificatur ecclesia*).[183] "The woman, therefore, is just as much God's creation as is the man. But, by her being made from the man, human unity (*unitas*) was commended to us; and by her being made in this way, as I said, Christ and the Church were prefigured."[184] The first parents prefigured the union of Christ and the church in anticipation of the perfect "unity" (*unitas*) and "fellowship" (*societas*) for which humanity was created. After the fall of the first parents, the two cities began to take shape among human beings in the figures of Abel and Cain. They represented "two cities, that is, two human societies (*societates*), one predestined to reign with God for all eternity," the other "to undergo eternal punishment with the devil."[185] The final, eschatological city will include all of the just who lived before the coming of Christ such as Abel, and all of the elect after Christ. Until the end time, the church mediates salvation by celebrating the sacraments. Baptism leads to the conversion of one city into another, and the Eucharist unites the "whole redeemed city, that is, the congregation and fellowship of the saints (*tota ipsa redempta civitas, hoc est congregatio societas que sanctorum*),"[186] as one sacrifice.[187] The church as the city of God on pilgrimage adds new citizens by celebrating the sacraments by which "believers are initiated (*quibus credentes initiantur*)."[188] This is the meaning and purpose of true religion found in the worship of Christians, not in the false worship of pagan gods. The church's role was to offer the true sacrifice of the whole Christ, head and members, as a body of charity and a means of grace for the transformation of the earthly city into the heavenly city.

Augustine's ecclesiology also took shape in his controversy with the Pelagians and in relation to his teachings on predestination and grace. In *To Simplician* (c. 396), Augustine argued that no good works merited grace. God did not give grace to those whom he foreknew would use grace well, for that would make grace dependent upon good works. Instead, God gave grace to those whom he willed, and any good deeds that led to salvation were gifts of grace. The paradigmatic instance of this principle could be found in Jacob and Esau, for Augustine argued upon his reading of Paul in Romans 9:13 that God freely chose Jacob rather than Esau. God did not choose Jacob because he foreknew Jacob would do good deeds, rather, God gave Jacob the grace to do good works. Jacob was a figure of the elect, who must be given an upright will in order to do the good.[189] Adam and Eve enjoyed a distinctive kind of freedom, but after their free rejection of God, all human beings share in the guilt and consequences of original sin. This meant that human freedom was fallen and could not will itself to God without grace. Only the elect who have been predestined to be conformed to the image of the Son (Rom. 8:29) will form the final communion of charity, the one church united in love.

While this represented a development in Augustine's thought on the relationship between grace, merit, and human freedom, it did not contradict his theology of the church, for as we have seen, he was committed to predestination while writing and preaching against the Donatists. The grace given to the elect was the very gift of charity that united the members as the one body of Christ. This was the work of the Spirit, and such grace was necessary in order for sinful human beings to share in charity. In his later works against the Pelagians, Augustine argued that grace was necessary not only for conversion, but also for perseverance to the end. The elect were given this grace, but no one could be assured that one was elect. God graciously redeems some, but others he permits to remain in their sin, namely, the reprobate.

Augustine's doctrine of predestination did not render the visible church ineffective or unnecessary, for the Catholic Church continued to mediate the grace of God by means of the sacraments. The church's mixed condition as a body of good and wicked, elect and reprobate, meant that no one could presume upon salvation as a member of the elect. This protected against the sins of pride, presumption, and complacency. One had to trust in the grace, mediated by the sacraments of the church, to unite one to the saints and to effect a gradual but definite transformation in love by cooperation with grace. Yet even this cooperation with grace was itself a gift of grace, given to those whom God had predestined to be joined to the bond of charity. Augustine's mature teachings on predestination and grace were intended to encourage Christians to place their hope in God's salvific work and not in their own efforts. A Christian's ultimate hope was found in the work of Christ and the Holy Spirit to bind the church in the unbreakable bond of charity.

NO SALVATION OUTSIDE OF THE CHURCH

Did Augustine teach a doctrine of "no salvation outside of the church"?[190] Like Cyprian, Augustine held that charity was a gift from the Holy Spirit that was necessary for salvation. There was no salvation apart from charity.[191] Unlike Cyprian, however, Augustine argued that the presence and activity of the Spirit was not determined by the bishop's union with the episcopal college. Charity could be found among the bishops, but it was not dependent upon them. Peter represented the whole church's unity in charity, not merely the bishop's unity with the episcopal college.[192]

According to Augustine, Christ was the one mediator whose salvific work was mediated by the one church. The unity of the church was constituted by unity in charity, in the Holy Spirit, and in Christ. Like Tertullian, Augustine understood that the work of the Holy Spirit applied to the whole church, laity and clergy alike. This was the same charity mediated by the visible church and the sacraments. Baptism transformed the carnal into the spiritual ones. Some might come to share in charity without having received the baptismal ritual of the Catholic Church, such as the martyrs who were baptized in their blood. Did this mean that baptism was unnecessary? Not at all, for all who came to share in charity did so by virtue of relation to the same charity mediated by baptism. This baptism could take different forms, such as baptism by blood. Even those who were not martyred were saved in some way by baptism, for those who wished to make progress in comprehending what belonged to the Spirit of God but died before becoming spiritual were "safeguarded by the holiness of the sacrament and are counted among the inhabitants of the living, where the Lord is our hope and portion."[193] The Holy Spirit could work outside of the visible church's sacraments, but always to bring those outside into the same unity of charity mediated by the sacraments of the Catholic Church. Thus, according to Augustine, there was no salvation outside of the church constituted by the bond of charity given by the Holy Spirit.

CONCLUSION

In Augustine's ecclesiology, the church is one and holy because of the work of the Holy Spirit. The failures and sins of the members did not compromise the church's holiness. The efficacy of the sacraments did not depend upon the minister, for the power belonged to God. However, the wicked who administered or received the sacraments unworthily cut themselves off from charity.

Against Cyprian, Augustine argued that schismatic bishops did not lose the sanctifying power to celebrate the sacraments. Baptism could be administered outside of the Catholic Church. Against the Donatists, Augustine declared that even apostate bishops could celebrate the sacraments, even though he maintained that Caecilian and his consecrators were innocent.[194] The church was holy because of the work of the Holy Spirit to unite the members of the body in the invisible union of charity. Augustine followed Tertullian in his understanding of charity as a gift given to clergy and laity alike. The church's sacraments had efficacy because of the whole Christ, head and members, whose charity forgave sins and united the one body. Unlike Tertullian, Augustine did not demand that those guilty of serious sins be permanently excluded from the church. While Tertullian held that the church did not have the power to forgive grave sins, Augustine believed that the only unforgivable sin was to be unrepentant and to cut oneself off from the unity of the body, the very error of schismatics. In addition, Tertullian gave primacy to the spiritual members with special charisms such as prophecy or miracles[195] over the clergy who sometimes erred in judgment. Augustine affirmed the bishop's authority to govern and to determine the proper penitential process to reconcile sinners. The church was not polluted by having sinners in her midst, for the love of the Holy Spirit could tolerate all things. Instead, the presence of the wicked purified the good members, enabling them to grow in patience and forbearance, while providing the opportunity for the conversion of sinners. Augustine thus offered a more inclusive view of the church than Tertullian since ecclesial membership was open to penitents and to all those united in charity. The church's mixed condition was willed by God to allow for the purification of the good and final separation from the wicked at the end time. All of the elect would be joined to the one unity in charity given by the Spirit and mediated by the sacraments of the Catholic Church.

Augustine relied upon theological claims from Tertullian, Cyprian, Tyconius, and Optatus in order to construct his rich and sophisticated theology of the church. The church was constituted by the members of the body of Christ, united in charity as a gift of the Holy Spirit. Participation in this body was mediated by the Catholic Church, but the Spirit could work beyond visible limits to join those outside of the church to the one invisible union in charity. This did not invalidate the sacraments, but only underscored the power of Christ and the Spirit to bring together the city of God from all nations. There was no salvation outside of the church because there was no salvation outside of the one Christ, head and members. The Catholic Church mediated salvation and holiness to the world as the body of Christ, albeit in a mixed and imperfect condition. Nevertheless, there was only one church. Leo the Great built upon Augustine's ecclesiology while expanding upon the mediatory role of bishop of Rome as the visible head of the church and the spiritual head of the world.

NOTES

1. Augustine, *Bapt.* 5.27.38; 4.3.5.

2. Robert Louis Wilken observes, "This decree was a first but momentous step in the establishment of Christianity as the official religion of the Roman world. Significantly, it was issued by the emperor without consultation with the bishops. It was less an effort on the part of the Church to impose its beliefs on the society than a political gesture on the part of the emperor to bring about religious unity in a fractured empire. The consequences were far reaching, for the decree cemented the alliance between the Church and political power that had emerged since the years of Constantine's rule, and shaped Western civilization for the next fifteen hundred years;" *The First Thousand Years: A Global History of Christianity* (New Haven: Yale University Press, 2012), 130.

3. On the context of the Donatist controversy, see John Whitehouse, "The Scholarship of the Donatist Controversy," in *The Donatist Schism: Controversy and Contexts*, ed. Richard Miles (Liverpool: Liverpool University Press, 2016), 34–53.

4. Burns, Jensen, et al., *Christianity in Roman Africa*, 47–48.

5. Wilhite, *North African Christianity*, 214–17.

6. Augustine, *Bapt.* 3.18.23.

7. The Donatists, like Cyprian, did not see the baptism of schismatics or heretics as "rebaptism;" Wilhite, *North African Christianity*, 216.

8. For an overview, see Matthew Alan Gaumer, *Augustine's Cyprian: Authority in Roman Africa* (Leiden: Brill, 2016).

9. In *Conf.* 2.9.17, Augustine wrote about an unfriendly form of friendship with those who stole pears and derived pleasure from the theft itself.

10. Augustine, *Conf.* 5.6.10–10.18.

11. Augustine, *Conf.* 5.7.12–13; 7.2.3–5.7.

12. Augustine, *Conf.* 8.2.3–6.

13. Augustine, *Cresc.* 4.64.79; *Petil.* 3.16.19.

14. I offer an extended argument to demonstrate the shift in Augustine's thought from an emphasis upon the Platonic ideal of vision to a focus on the Biblical virtues of faith, hope, and charity in *Augustine and the Mystery of the Church* (Minneapolis: Fortress Press, 2017).

15. Augustine, *Conf.* 1.11.17; *Catech.* 26.50; *Pecc. merit.* 2.26.42. For an extended description of the catechumenate during Augustine's life, see William Harmless, *Augustine and the Catechumenate* (Collegeville: Liturgical Press, 1995).

16. Tertullian, *Bapt.* 7.1; 8.2; Augustine, *Serm. Dolb.* 26(198*).53; *Qu. eu.* 2.40.3.
17. Augustine, *Bapt.* 7.53.101–102.
18. Augustine, *Bapt.* 2.7.11; 5.23.33; *Serm.* 296.15.
19. Augustine frequently spoke of the church as *catholica* instead of *ecclesia*; Maureen Tilley, *The Donatist Controversy I* (WSA I/21), 20.
20. Augustine, *Bapt.* 1.1.2–2.3; 7.52.100.
21. Augustine, *Serm.* 227.12; 229.1; *Serm. Guelf.* 7(229A).1.
22. Augustine, *Eu. Io.* 26.15; 27.11; *Serm.* 272; *Serm. Guelf.* 7(229A).1. Augustine relied upon Cyprian for the understanding of the Eucharist as representing the whole Christ; Cyprian, *Ep.* 63.13.1–15; Burns, Jensen, et al., *Christianity in Roman Africa*, 277.
23. Augustine, *Serm.* 261.9; *Serm. Guelf.* 33(77A).4.
24. Augustine, *Serm. Dolb.* 18 (306E).7; *Serm. Guelf.* 33(77A).4; *Ep. Io.* 3.9.
25. Augustine, *Serm.* 9.3–4, 11; 392.3–5.
26. Augustine, *Ep.* 54.3.4.
27. Augustine, *Enchir.* 17.65.
28. Augustine, *Serm.* 232.8.
29. Augustine, *Enchir.* 17.65.
30. Burns, Jensen, et al., *Christianity in Roman Africa*, 341–43.
31. Augustine, *Ep.* 184.10.45.
32. Augustine, *Parm.* 2.13.28; *Bapt.* 1.1.2.
33. Augustine, *Serm.* 99.9.
34. Augustine, *Bapt.* 5.21.29.
35. Augustine, *Serm.* 295.5.5; 351.5.12; *Serm. Guelf.* 16(229N).2.
36. Augustine, *Serm.* 71.23.37; *Enchir.* 22.83.
37. Augustine, *Ep.* 153.3.7.
38. Augustine, *Serm. Dolb.* 26(198*).49–50.
39. Augustine, *Faust.* 11.2, 5; 13.5; 28.4; 33.9.
40. Burns, Jensen, et al., *Christianity in Roman Africa*, 428.
41. Augustine drew upon Optatus's view that the bishops and their clergy acted as agents of Christ and his ecclesial body, dispensing goods that were not theirs; Burns, Jensen, et al., *Christianity in Roman Africa*, 428, 609–10; Optatus, *Parm.* 2.10; 5.1, 4.
42. Augustine, *Gen. Man.* 2.13.19, 24.37.
43. Augustine, *Gen. Man.* 2.24.37; CSEL 91.161: "item reliquit et matrem, id est synagogae ueterem atque carnalem obseruationem, quae illi mater erat ex semine dauid secundum carnem, et adhaesit uxori suae, id est ecclesiae, ut sint duo in carne una. dicit enim apostolus ipsum esse caput ecclesiae, et ecclesiam corpus eius."
44. Augustine, *Gen. Man.* 2.24.37; CSEL 91.161: "ergo et ipse soporatus est dormitione passionis, ut ei coniux ecclesia formaretur, quam dormitionem cantat per prophetam dicens: ego dormiui, et somnum cepi; et exsurrexi, quoniam dominus suscepit me. formata est ergo ei coniux ecclesia de latere eius, id est de fide passionis et baptismi."
45. Augustine, *Gen. Man.* 2.24.37; *Faust.* 12.16; 12.20; 12.39; *Gen. litt.* 9.18; *Eu. Io.* 9.10; 15.8; 20.2; *Ciu.* 15.26; *Psal.* 56.11; 65.7; 126.7; 138.2; *Serm.* 336.5.
46. Augustine, *Quaest.* 36.2.
47. Augustine, *Doct. Chr.* 2.6.7.
48. Augustine, *Doct. Chr.* prol.6.
49. Augustine, *Doct. Chr.* prol.6; CCSL 32.4: "deinde ipsa caritas, quae sibi homines inuicem nodo unitatis adstringit."
50. Augustine, *Doct. Chr.* 1.16.15; CCSL 32.15: "est enim ecclesia corpus eius, sicut apostolica doctrina commendat, quae coniux etiam eius dicitur. corpus ergo suum multis membris diuersa officia gerentibus, nodo unitatis et caritatis tamquam sanitatis adstringit."
51. Augustine, *Doct. Chr.* 1.29.30; CCSL 32.23: "nos in societate dilectionis dei."
52. Augustine, *Doct. Chr.* 2.6.7.
53. Augustine, *Doct. Chr.* 2.6.7; CCSL 32.35: "qui boni fideles et ueri dei serui deponentes onera saeculi ad sanctum baptismi lauacrum uenerunt atque inde ascendentes conceptione sancti spiritus fructum dant geminae caritatis, id est dei et proximi."

54. Augustine, *Quaest.* 66; *Rom. prop.* 12.2, 7–12; 52.15; 53.7; 67.1–3; *Gal.* 3.2; 43.3; 44.3–5; 49.5–6; *Simpl.* 1.1.7–10.
55. Augustine, *Quaest.* 66.2–3, 5–6; *Rom. prop.* 12.10; 38.1, 7; 42.2; *Gal.* 22.7; 46.7.
56. Tyconius, *Reg.* regula secunda, septima; Augustine, *Doct. Chr.* 3.32.45, 37.55.
57. Augustine, *Faust.* 12.15; *Answer to Faustus*, trans. Roland Teske (WSA I/20), 136; *Ciu.* 15.26–27; 16.1–8; *Cat. rud.* 19.32; *Bapt.* 5.28.39.
58. Tertullian, *Idol.* 24.4; Rankin, *Tertullian and the Church*, 66.
59. Rankin, *Tertullian and the Church*, 66.
60. Augustine, *Faust.* 12.16.
61. Augustine, *Faust.* 12.14; Teske, *Answer to Faustus* (WSA I/20), 135.
62. Augustine, *Faust.* 12.14; 13.16; 17.6; 32.18.
63. Augustine, *Faust.* 12.15; Teske, *Answer to Faustus* (WSA I/20), 136.
64. Augustine, *Trin.* 7.3.6; *Serm.* 71.33; *Eu. Io.* 9.8.
65. Michael Root, "Augustine on the Church," in *T&T Clark Companion to Augustine and Modern Theology*, eds. C. C. Pecknold and T. Toom (New York: Bloomsbury T&T Clark, 2013), 62.
66. Optatus, *Parm.* 7.3.
67. Augustine, *Serm.* 71.33.
68. Augustine, *Ep. Io.* 3.5.
69. Root, "Augustine on the Church," 62.
70. Augustine, *Faust.* 12.8.
71. Augustine, *Faust.* 12.14.
72. Augustine, *Faust.* 12.15.
73. Augustine, *Cat. rud.* 27.53; *Instructing Beginners in Faith*, trans. Raymond Canning (New York: New City Press, 2006), 168; *Cat. rud.* 19.32; *Faust.* 12.14–23; *Ciu.* 15.26–27; 16.1–8.
74. Augustine, *Faust.* 12.20; Teske, *Answer to Faustus* (WSA I/20), 138; CSEL 25.349: "quo significaret nonnullos etiam extra ecclesiam baptizatos, si eis pinguedo non defuerit caritatis, posteriore tempore quasi uespere in ore columbae tamquam in osculo pacis ad unitatis societatem posse perduci."
75. Augustine, *Faust.* 12.20; Teske, *Answer to Faustus* (WSA I/20), 138; CSEL 25.349: "quod post alios septem dies dimissa reuersa non est, significat finem saeculi, quando erit sanctorum requies, non adhuc in sacramento spei, quo in hoc tempore consociatur ecclesia, quamdiu bibitur, quod de christi latere manauit, sed iam in ipsa perfectione salutis aeternae, cum tradetur regnum deo et patri, ut in illa perspicua contemplatione incommutabilis ueritatis nullis mysteriis corporalibus egeamus."
76. Augustine, *Faust.* 13.16.
77. Augustine, *Faust.* 12.17; 12.20.
78. Augustine, *Faust.* 12.22; 12.20.
79. Augustine, *Faust.* 12.42.
80. Augustine, *Doct. Chr.* 1.16.15.
81. Augustine, *Faust.* 15.3.
82. Augustine, *Faust.* 15.3–11.
83. Augustine, *Faust.* 13.14.
84. Augustine, *Faust.* 13.13.
85. Augustine, *Faust.* 12.26–28.
86. Augustine, *Faust.* 12.36; Teske, *Answer to Faustus* (WSA I/20), 148.
87. Augustine, *Faust.* 12.26.
88. Augustine, *Faust.* 12.8, 26.
89. Augustine, *Faust.* 13.16; 15.4.
90. Augustine, *Faust.* 12.14; Teske, *Answer to Faustus* (WSA I/20), 135.
91. The first two books were written in 400, while the third was written in 403.
92. Augustine, *Petil.* 1.5.6–7.8; 3.52.64.
93. Augustine, *Petil.* 1.5.6.
94. Augustine, *Petil.* 3.49.59.
95. Augustine, *Petil.* 3.49.59.

96. Augustine, *Petil.* 2.33.78.
97. Optatus held that the two constant and unchanging elements in baptism were the invocation of the Trintiy and the faith of the recipient; Optatus, *Parm.* 2.10; 5.1, 4; Burns, Jensen, et al., *Christianity in Roman Africa*, 609–10.
98. Augustine, *Petil.* 2.22.50.
99. Augustine, *Petil.* 2.3.6.
100. Augustine, *Petil.* 2.31.71.
101. Augustine offers a creative etymology for the Greek *katholon* to mean "according to the whole;" Augustine, *Petil.* 2.38.91.
102. Augustine, *Parm.* 3.2.8–11; 3.4.25.
103. Augustine, *Parm.* 2.11.23–24.
104. Augustine, *Parm.* 2.13.29; Tilley, *The Donatist Controversy I* (WSA I/21), 326.
105. Augustine, *Parm.* 2.13.28.
106. Augustine, *Parm.* 2.13.28.
107. Augustine, *Bapt.* 1.18.28.
108. Augustine, *Bapt.* 2.4.5; Geoffrey Dunn, "Augustine's Use of the Pauline Portrayal of Peter in Galatians 2," *Augustinian Studies* 46:1 (2015): 37.
109. Augustine, *Bapt.* 1.10.13.
110. Augustine, *Bapt.* 1.12.19.
111. Augustine, *Bapt.* 1.12.19.
112. Augustine, *Bapt.* 1.14.22.
113. Augustine, *Bapt.* 1.10.13.
114. Augustine, *Bapt.* 1.10.13.
115. Augustine, *Bapt.* 1.15.23.
116. Augustine, *Bapt.* 1.15.23; CSEL 51.167: "prior autem fuit ishmael et postea isaac, et prior esau, posterior autem iacob, non quia prior peperit haeresis quam ecclesia aut ipsa ecclesia prius carnales uel animales et postea spiritales, sed quia in ipsa sorte mortalitatis nostrae ex quo de adam nascimur non est prius quod spiritale sed quod animale, postea spiritale. ex ipso autem animali sensu, quia homo animalis non percipit quae sunt spiritus dei, omnes dissensiones et schismata generantur."
117. Augustine, *Bapt.* 1.15.24; CSEL 51.168: "ecclesia uero quod est populus dei etiam in istius uitae peregrinatione antiqua res est, in aliis hominibus habens animalem portionem, in aliis autem spiritalem."
118. Augustine, *Bapt.* 1.15.24; CSEL 51.168: "ad animales pertinet uetus testamentum, ad spiritales nouum. sed primis temporibus utrumque occultum fuit ab adam usque ad moysen. a moyse autem manifestatum est uetus et in eo ipso occultabatur nouum, quia occulte significabatur. postea uero quam in carne dominus uenit reuelatum est nouum."
119. On the relationship between the *sacramenta* of the old covenant and the *sacramenta* of Christ, see Augustine, *Faust.* 19.11–17; Lee, *Mystery of the Church*, 16–21.
120. Augustine, *Bapt.* 1.16.25.
121. Augustine, *Faust.* 19.13–14.
122. Augustine, *Faust.* 19.13–14.
123. Augustine, *Bapt.* 1.17.26.
124. Augustine, *Bapt.* 4.17.24.
125. Augustine, *Bapt.* 3.16.21; Cyprian, *Ep.* 73.6.2.
126. Augustine, *Bapt.* 3.16.21.
127. Augustine, *Bapt.* 3.16.21–17.22.
128. Augustine, *Bapt.* 3.17.22.
129. Augustine, *Bapt.* 3.18.23; CSEL 51.214–15: "ergo si personam gerebant ecclesiae et sic eis hoc dictum est, tamquam ipsi ecclesiae diceretur, pax ecclesiae dimittit peccata et ab ecclesiae pace alienatio tenet peccata non secundum arbitrium hominum, sed secundum arbitrium dei et orationes sanctorum spiritalium, qui omnia iudicant, ipsi autem a nemine diiudicantur."
130. Augustine, *Bapt.* 3.18.23.
131. Augustine, *Ep.* 53.2.

132. Augustine, *Bapt.* 3.18.23; Tilley, *The Donatist Controversy I* (WSA I/21), 457; CSEL 51.215: "pax autem huius unitatis in solis bonis est uel iam spiritalibus uel ad spiritalia concordi oboedientia proficientibus; in malis autem non est, siue foris tumultuentur siue intus cum gemitu tolerentur et baptizent et baptizentur."

133. While it is not always clear who is among the dove or the saints, Augustine says that at times, not only does God know how removed some are from the perfection and unity of the dove, even humans can see how wicked some are, but the final separation will take place openly at the end; Augustine, *Bapt.* 4.13.20.

134. Augustine, *Bapt.* 4.3.4.

135. Augustine, *Bapt.* 5.27.38.

136. Augustine, *Bapt.* 5.27.38; Tilley, *The Donatist Controversy I* (WSA I/21), 528.

137. Augustine, *Bapt.* 5.27.38; Tilley, *The Donatist Controversy I* (WSA I/21), 529.

138. Augustine, *Bapt.* 5.23.33.

139. Augustine, *Bapt.* 4.13.19; 6.2.4–4.6. Geoffrey Dunn observes that Augustine's position would later be described as the principle of *ex opere operato*; "Augustine's Use of the Pauline Portrayal of Peter in Galatians 2," *Augustinian Studies* 46:1 (2015): 35.

140. Augustine, *Bapt.* 3.18.23; 5.21.29, 23.33; 6.4.6–5.7.

141. Cyprian, *Ep.* 73.7.2.

142. Augustine, *Bapt.* 3.18.23.

143. Augustine, *Bapt.* 4.9.13.

144. Augustine, *Ep. Io.* 1.2; 2.2; *Psal.* 44.3; 148.8; *Serm.* 161.1; *Serm. Dolb.* 26(198*).43.

145. Augustine, *Serm. Dolb.* 22(341*).2, perhaps delivered in 417; Dolbeau 554.24–25: "totus christus in plenitudine ecclesiae." Augustine most often speaks of the whole Christ in his *Sermons*; Burns, Jensen, et al., *Christianity in Roman Africa*, 615n85.

146. Christ the head remains the source of grace to the members of the body; *Eu. Io.* 82.3; 13.8; 15.31; 21.8; *Ep. Io.* 6.10; 10.3; *Cresc.* 2.13.16; *Agon.* 20.22; *Psal.* 29[2].2; 21[2].28; 41.1; 90[2].1; *Serm.* 62.3.

147. Augustine, *Serm. Dolb.* 22(341*).2–11; *Psal.* 36[3].4; 62.2; 138.2.

148. Augustine, *Conf.* 13.34.49; *Confessions*, trans. Maria Boulding (WSA I/1), 305; *Serm.* 229S; *Psal.* 3.9.

149. Michael Fiedrowicz, *Psalmus vox totius Christi: Studien zu Augustins 'Enarrationes in Psalmos'* (Freiburg: Herder, 1997), 15, 298–375; Michael Cameron, *Christ Meets Me Everywhere* (New York: Oxford University Press, 2012), 171–212.

150. Augustine, *Psal.* 30[3].1.

151. Augustine, *Psal.* 30[2].4; 40.6; 140.6; 101[1].2; 118[22].5.

152. Augustine, *Psal.* 30[2].3; 90[2].5.

153. Augustine, *Psal.* 30[2].3; *Expositions of the Psalms 1–32*, trans. Maria Boulding (WSA III/15), 323; CCSL 38.192: "nam sine illo, nos nihil; in illo autem, ipse christus et nos. quare? quia totus christus caput et corpus. caput ille saluator corporis, qui iam adscendit in caelum; corpus autem ecclesia, quae laborat in terra. hoc autem corpus nisi connexione caritatis adhaereret capiti suo, ut unus fieret ex capite et corpore, non de caelo quemdam persecutorem corripiens diceret: saule, saule, quid me persequeris?" Augustine, *Psal.* 37.6; 142.3; *Serm.* 345.4.

154. Augustine, *Psal.* 26.1; 37.6; 85.1; *Serm.* 129.4.

155. Augustine, *Psal.* 62.2; *Expositions of the Psalms 51–72*, trans. Maria Boulding (WSA III/17), 230.

156. Augustine, *Psal.* 90[2].5; 61.4.

157. Augustine, *Psal.* 30[2].3.

158. Augustine, *Psal.* 26[2].11; Boulding, *Expositions of the Psalms 1–32* (WSA III/15), 282.

159. Michael Cameron, "Transfiguration: Christology and the Roots of Figurative Exegesis in St. Augustine," *Studia Patristica* 33 (1997): 40–47.

160. Augustine, *Serm.* 4.11; *Psal.* 36[3].4; 128.2; *Cat. rud.* 17.28; *Ciu.* 7.32; 10.25; 16.2; 18.23, 47; David Meconi, *The One Christ: St. Augustine's Theology of Deification* (Washington, DC: Catholic University of America Press, 2013), 186.

161. Augustine, *Serm. Dolb.* 22(341*).19; *Psal.* 64.2; 90[2].1; 128.2; *Ciu.* 15.7.

162. Augustine, *Psal.* 36[3].4; 128. 2; *Serm.* 341.9, 11; *Cat. rud.* 3.6; 17.28; *Ciu.* 7.32; 10.25; 16.2; 18.23, 47.
163. Augustine, *Faust.* 19.16; 20.21; 22.17.
164. Augustine, *Serm.* 350.3; *Faust.* 12.9; 22.17; *Ep. Io.* 5.8; *Psal.* 48[2].11; *Ciu.* 15.1.
165. Why did Augustine choose Abel as the beginning of the pilgrim church rather than Adam? David Meconi argues that Abel presented a unique case since there was no account of his personal sin in the Scriptures. Some followers of Pelagius viewed Abel as an example of human sinlessness, however, Augustine turned to Abel in order to show that the church is not a place for the inviolable but rather for sinners since all have sinned in Adam; Meconi, *The One Christ*, 188–91.
166. Augustine, *Psal.* 64.2; 86.6; *Ciu.* 14.28.
167. Augustine, *Psal.* 61.8; 64.2; 86.6; 136.1–12.
168. Augustine, *Psal.* 61.9; 86.6–7; Lee, *Augustine and the Mystery of the Church*, 84–88.
169. Augustine, *Psal.* 61.6–-8; 70.2; 136.12.
170. Augustine, *Psal.* 61.8.
171. Augustine, *Psal.* 77.22–23; 93.9, 15; *Bapt.* 4.9.12; *Faust.* 13.16; *Cat. rud.* 25.48.
172. Augustine, *Psal.* 126.3.
173. Augustine, *Psal.* 61.6.
174. Augustine, *Serm.* 267.4; 268.2.
175. Augustine, *Eu. Io.* 26.15; *Homilies on First John*, trans. Boniface Ramsey (WSA III/13), 463.
176. Augustine, *Serm.* 355.2; *Serm. Dolb.* 26(198*).48.
177. Augustine, *Serm.* 107.1.2; 265.9.11.
178. Augustine, *Serm.* 9.21; 25.8; 38.8; 86.3.3; 239.5.6–6.7; 354.4.
179. Augustine, *Serm.* 359.9; *Psal.* 32[2].2.29.
180. See John C. Cavadini, "Ideology and Solidarity in Augustine's *City of God*," in *Augustine's* City of God: *A Critical Guide*, ed. James Wetzel (New York: Cambridge University Press, 2012), 93–110.
181. Augustine, *Ciu.* 10.6.
182. Augustine, *Ciu.* 12.28; *The City of God*, trans. William Babcock (WSA I/7), 66; CCSL 48.384: "quem propterea deus creare uoluit unum, de quo multitudo propagaretur, ut hac admonitione etiam in multis concors unitas servaretur. quod uero femina illi ex eius latere facta est, etiam hic satis significatum est quam cara mariti et uxoris debeat esse coniunctio."
183. Augustine, *Ciu.* 22.17; CCSL 48.836.
184. Augustine, *Ciu.* 22.17; Babcock, *The City of God* (WSA I/7), 527; CCSL 48.836: "creatura est ergo dei femina sicut uir; sed ut de uiro fieret, unitas commendata; ut autem illo modo fieret, christus, ut dictum est, et ecclesia figurata est."
185. Augustine, *Ciu.* 15.1; Babcock, *The City of God* (WSA I/7), 139; CCL 48.453: "quas etiam mystice appellamus ciuitates duas, hoc est duas societates hominum, quarum est una quae praedestinata est in aeternum regnare cum deo, altera aeternum supplicium subire cum diabolo."
186. Augustine, *Ciu.* 10.6; Babcock, *The City of God* (WSA I/6), 311; CCSL 47.279: "profecto efficitur, ut tota ipsa redempta ciuitas, hoc est congregatio societas que sanctorum, uniuersale sacrificium offeratur deo per sacerdotem magnum, qui etiam se ipsum obtulit in passione pro nobis, ut tanti capitis corpus essemus, secundum formam serui."
187. Augustine, *Ciu.* 10.20; 10.6.
188. Augustine, *Ciu.* 15.26: "And as for the door that was cut in its side, it is clearly the wound that was made when the Crucified's side was pierced by the spear. This is plainly the way of entrance for those who come to him, for from that wound flowed the sacraments by which believers are initiated"; Babcock, *The City of God* (WSA I/7), 179; CCSL 48.494: "et quod ostium in latere accepit, profecto illud est uulnus, quando latus crucifixi lancea perforatum est; hac quippe ad illum uenientes ingrediuntur, quia inde sacramenta manarunt, quibus credentes initiantur."
189. Augustine, *Simpl.* 1.2.3.
190. Augustine, *Bapt.* 4.17.24; CSEL 51.250: "salus extra ecclesiam non est;" Cyprian, *Ep.* 73.21.2.

191. Augustine, *Bapt.* 4.17.24.
192. Augustine, *Serm.* 67.2.3; 76.1.1; 149.6.7–7.8; 232.2; 295.5.2.
193. Augustine, *Bapt.* 1.15.24.
194. Imperial records showed that the consecrator of Caecilian had been falsely accused; Burns, Jensen, et al., *Christianity in Roman Africa*, 610n61.
195. Augustine reports that many miracles were worked during his time; Augustine, *Ciu.* 22.8.

Chapter Four

Leo the Great

Pope Leo the Great (c. 400–461) became the bishop of Rome in 440 during a time of adversity in the West and theological controversy with the East. He inherited a church in a city that had been battered by barbarian invasions and struggled to maintain social order. While Leo distinguished between the two realms of church and empire, he saw them as partners whose interests went hand in hand. Writing to the imperial rulers, Leo argued that the peace and temporal prosperity of the empire was linked directly to the peace and unity of the church.[1] As the bishop of Rome, Leo sought to make Christianity the civic religion by introducing a new liturgical calendar of feasts and by enhancing papal influence in the socio-political sphere.[2] While attempting to bring church and society together, Leo also worked to overcome division between Western and Eastern Christian communities. This was most evident in his contributions to the Christological controversy in the fifth century. Although Leo has often been called the doctor of Christian unity, he was unable to establish lasting unity between the Western and Eastern churches.[3] Nevertheless, Leo played an important role in constructing a Western ecclesiology that emphasized papal authority and the Catholic Church's mediation of salvation to all people.

THE LIFE OF LEO THE GREAT

Very little is known of Leo prior to his ministry in the church. According to one source, he was born near the end of the fourth century in Tuscany, while another locates his upbringing in Volaterrae.[4] Leo's writings demonstrate an education in Latin rhetoric and prose, but they give no evidence of an advanced classical education with allusions to pagan literature as seen in the works of Tertullian and Augustine. This meant that Leo was educated exclusively as a Christian. He served as an acolyte for the Roman church and came to the attention of Augustine.[5] In 418, Leo was tasked with delivering a letter to Aurelius of Carthage in North Africa in which the presbyter Sixtus condemned the teachings of Pelagius. During the papacy of Caelestine (422–432), Leo was promoted to the office of archdeacon of Rome, in which capacity he administered church finances, organized charity to the poor, sent messages between imperial courts and the apostolic see, and assisted the pope.[6] Leo was also sent on diplomatic missions to establish alliances between secular powers and the ecclesiastical administration. He was consecrated priest and bishop of Rome in September 440. As part of his first duties, he regulated the readmission of those guilty of Pelagianism into the church. Leo maintained his commitment to the Augustinian view of grace and his fidelity to Augustine's teachings. Leo also had to deal with Manichaens who had fled to Rome after the Vandal invasion of North Africa. A trial was held in Rome, the results of which led to the burning of Manichaen books and the banishment of those who refused to recant.

By the middle of the fifth century, in the absence of strong leadership by the emperor or Senate, the bishop of Rome came to play an increasingly important role in civic affairs.[7] The impact of hostile invasions, migration, and the permanent settlement of barbarians was felt acutely in Rome. Roman food supplies from North Africa were cut off after the Vandal invasions, resulting in a major loss of grain and oil. Rome also faced the threat of invasion by the Vandals and the Huns. Leo was famously part of a delegation that negotiated a truce with Attila in Venetia.[8] The growth of papal power during Leo's pontificate was also influenced by the weakness of the Western emperor, Valentinian III, who was proclaimed Augustus at Rome in 425 at the age of 6. After a turbulent reign and his murder at the hands of his bodyguards in 455, there was a period of instability in the imperial regime. With the decline of the Roman empire, the Roman bishop came to prominence, which Leo understood as part of God's providence. Leo believed that God had chosen Rome in order to bring Christianity to the world.

During Leo's papacy, he expanded the reach of papal authority and jurisdiction. He began to exercise disciplinary measures and rules for provinces in North Africa in order to provide a unified set of legal guidelines for bishops to resolve issues. Whatever Leo's motivations, it was clear that the bishop of Rome exercised increasing jurisdiction over the church as a whole.

This was also evident in Leo's relationship to the Eastern churches, which followed a more democratic model of episcopal authority. These churches recognized the authority of the bishop of Rome within the larger context of an ecumenical council called by the emperor. This was on display with the case of Eutyches and the Christological controversy in the middle of the fifth century. At the outbreak of the Christological controversy in the East, the emperor Theodosius invited Leo to provide support for his position. Leo intervened in the controversy by commissioning a simple statement that affirmed the Western view of Christ as two natures in a single *persona*. Christ is both God and man, and therefore mediator. In June 449, Leo sent this statement, known as Leo's *Tome*, to a synod of bishops as a sign of his Petrine authority. The church of Peter and Paul was predestined by God for leadership in the universal church, with jurisdiction not only over Rome but over every church. The *Tome* manifested Rome's teaching authority over the churches of the East. It also provided a firm Western Christological doctrine that rejected the heresy of Eutyches and proved to be highly influential, although it was not immediately well-received in the East.

After a series of controversial gatherings of bishops and clergy, eventually a negotiation between Rome and the Eastern court led to the council of Chalcedon in 451,which seemed to affirm the main lines of Leo's *Tome*. As a result, Leo claimed an important victory. The bishop of Rome rightly possessed magisterial authority over the church, and he served as a visible sign of ecclesial unity.

In addition to these internal struggles, Leo was faced with external pressures. After the deaths of the emperors Valentinian and Maximus, the city of Rome was captured by the Vandals in 455. As a result, Leo had to melt down 600 pounds of silver in order to pay ransom and tribute to barbarian invaders. The church in Rome was faced with economic struggles for the rest of Leo's reign, and he also became preoccupied with Egyptian opposition to Chalcedonian Christology, a division that was stoked by the new emperor Leo I (457–474). Leo died without having resolved these internal and external problems in 461. He was buried at St. Peter's and has been honored as a saint in both the West and the East.

THE CHURCH IN ROME

Leo understood the church in Rome as predestined for leadership. Just as Rome, the eternal city, had played an essential role in the spread of the empire, so too the see of Peter possessed a distinctive identity as head of the church. Rome had claimed to be the eternal city, yet it had fallen to the Goths in 410 and to the Vandals in 452. Despite its political struggles, Rome was established as a symbol of the headship of the empire and the world, a headship that belonged spiritually to the bishop of Rome. Scholars have noted that Leo did not simply accept a *romanitas* in which Roman culture and institutions were bound together by a political ideology that sought to expand the imperial regime by adopting the pagan virtues.[9] After all, those virtues had failed to protect Rome from barbarian invasions. Instead, influenced by Augustine's understanding of the city of God, Leo offered a new vision of the world based upon his theology of ecclesiastical unity. According to Augustine, the church was the heavenly city of God on pilgrimage through this world, and the citizens of the heavenly city were in exile in Babylon. They were intermingled with the earthly city until the final separation of the cities at the end time. In Leo's view, the love of God and the love of the world were opposed to each other, and the church could claim to be the true eternal city, through which the Gospel would be carried to the ends of the earth.

The bishop's responsibilities by the time of Leo's entrance into the ecclesiastical hierarchy looked similar to those in the third and fourth centuries. The bishop was responsible for a number of pastoral and civic duties. He was tasked with governing churches within his jurisdiction and controlling revenues, administering the sacraments and reconciling penitents, ordaining priests and deacons, instructing the faithful and correcting heretics, supervising monks and clergy, participating in synods, offering and organizing charitable care for the needy in society (widows, orphans, and the poor), and settling some secular disputes as judge and arbitrator.[10] The bishop celebrated the eucharistic liturgy and regularly performed baptisms, although priests also carried out these sacramental celebrations on behalf of the bishop if he was unable to be present. During this period, it belonged to the bishop alone to reconcile penitents and to determine appropriate penitential measures.

In terms of ecclesiastical administration, the Western hierarchy in the fifth century was somewhat fluid with regard to formal structures. In general, the boundaries of secular prefectures, dioceses, and provinces corresponded to ecclesial boundaries, although Christian leaders adamantly denied that the church could be subject to divisions made by the empire.[11] In Italy, just as there were two dioceses comprising southern and northern territories, so there were two ecclesiastical divisions. The bishop of Rome was responsible for the south, which had no metropolitans since it was never a province, while the bishop of Milan was the metropolitan for the rest of Italy. The physical boundaries of ecclesiastical divisions were not always clear, and in a departure from the secular model, the function of the office was circumscribed according to its place in the hierarchy. The office of bishop was divided into categories, with the highest rank being the archbishop or patriarch of the major sees of Rome, Constantinople, Alexandria, Antioch, and Jerusalem, while next in rank was the metropolitan in charge of an entire province. The metropolitan was elected by the bishops of the province, and his responsibilities were disciplinary and supervisory. A bishop's sphere of activity was restricted to his immediate jurisdiction, which emphasized the relative importance of the metropolitans and patriarchs. Leo extended papal jurisdiction in areas such as Gaul and North Africa so that by the end of his pontificate, Rome played a central role in settling ecclesial disputes among bishops.[12]

In addition to the bishop's pastoral and spiritual obligations, the bishop's charity and care for the poor was the means by which he participated in the wider social community. Further, by the fifth century, the bishop was sometimes asked to intervene in secular courts and to defend the city in the midst of the threat of invasions. Leo took on these responsibilities while also emphasizing the spiritual leadership of the Roman bishop, even founding a monastery at St. Peter's basilica. Leo's theology of the church is discernible in his preaching and in his letters of correspondence that survive.

LEO'S WORKS

Leo's extant body of writings consisted of 97 *Sermons* and 143 *Letters*. His letters were concerned not only with doctrinal but also disciplinary and judicial matters, and many have been utilized in canon law. His 143 letters constituted the largest surviving papal letter collection before the time of Gregory the Great.

Leo's sermons were characterized by simple eloquence and particular attention to Christian charity. Unlike his predecessors and contemporaries, Leo did not regularly engage in allegorical exegesis of the Scriptures but instead preferred clarity of interpretation in order to teach Christian doctrine. Leo's teaching on the nature of the church took shape in the midst of his ecclesiastical, civic, and theological disputes. He relied upon traditional images of the church found in earlier authors and in the Scriptures. Although he drew upon Augustine's theology, he offered his own vision of the church's unity, holiness, and Catholic apostolicity.

IMAGES OF THE CHURCH

Like his Latin predecessors, Leo's theology of the church was built upon an incarnational Christology. Following Augustine, Leo held that Christ came and took on human flesh and soul in the womb of the virgin mother, not thereby decreasing the divine but rather increasing the human by the divine.[13] Baptism enabled those born in Adam to be reborn in Christ, thereby sharing in Christ's human nature so as to be united as one body.[14] Because of the mystery of the incarnation, Christ the head and the members of his body the church can be united as one flesh (Gen. 2:24), one body from the union of bridegroom and bride. The church was born from Christ's side on the cross, from which water and blood flowed as signs of the sacraments, particularly baptism.[15] The union of the divine and human natures form one Christ. According to Leo, this was the content of the true faith that "makes us true Christians," for this Christology enabled human beings to be joined to the human nature of Christ and to be united to the Godhead.[16] When the Word took on our flesh, our nature was united to his unchangeable substance, that is, his divinity.[17] The complete union of the divine and human in the womb of the virgin made possible the church's participation in divinity. Eutyches made the error of denying the real human flesh of Jesus in his faulty Christology (even if Eutyches did not think so himself), which rendered void the mystery of salvation.[18] The whole church has received the fullness of the Godhead bodily, as the body clinging to the head whose flesh was real.[19] Those who denied the doctrine of God's church have placed themselves outside of the body of Christ.[20] Christology has ecclesiological and soteriological consequences, and a proper Christology is essential for salvation.

According to Leo, Christ has provided the church with an example of human perfection. "For unless he were true God, he would not bring us a remedy, unless he were true man, he would not give us an example."[21] Following Augustine's teaching, Leo argued that Christ's human nature offered an example that could be followed and that enabled a Christian to become "a partner in the divine nature" as the body of Christ the head.[22] Christians must love what Christ loved so as to find the grace of God and to love God in one's neighbor.[23] The sacrament of baptism made Christians into the temple of the Holy Spirit.[24] Christ's conception by the Holy Spirit and his birth from the virgin mother by the Holy Spirit made possible the spiritual conception of the church and the birth of salvation for the human race.[25] "Since, as the Lord Jesus became our flesh by being born, so we also became his body by being reborn. Therefore are we both members of Christ, and the temple of the Holy Ghost."[26] Having been reborn by the Spirit of God and having received grace in order to become the son of God by the spirit of adoption, the Christian can call God Father.[27]

Leo understood the Spirit as the mother of the church's unity. Just as the Holy Spirit brought forth the son of God in the incarnation, so too the Spirit has brought forth the sons of God as the "nurse of love and the mother of unity," whose proper work is "to join to God those whom it removes from the world."[28] The same Holy Spirit who filled the virgin has filled the font of baptism.[29] The Holy Spirit can be identified as the Spirit of Christ,[30] for the persons of the Trinity were distinct but united in action.

> For the majesty of the Holy Ghost is never separate from the omnipotence of the Father and the Son, and whatever the divine government accomplishes in the ordering of all things, proceeds from the providence of the whole Trinity. Therein exists unity of mercy and loving-kindness, unity of judgment and justice: nor is there any division in action where there is no divergence of will.[31]

The ultimate source of the church's unity is the Trinity, and those who have not received the wisdom and teaching of the Holy Spirit are not members of Christ's body and cannot glory in Christ the head.[32] Not only has the Holy

Spirit led the church into all truth (John 16:12–15), the Spirit has sanctified the whole church.[33] The Holy Spirit established the church's practices of fasting and almsgiving.[34] According to Leo, the Spirit must be manifested not in charisms such as prophecy and miracles, but rather in almsgiving and love for the poor. The practices of prayer, fasting, and almsgiving have united the members of the church to the Holy Spirit.

> For by prayer we seek to propitiate God, by fasting we extinguish the lusts of the flesh, by alms we redeem our sins: and at the same time God's image is throughout renewed in us, if we are always ready to praise Him, unfailingly intent on our purification and unceasingly active in cherishing our neighbor. This threefold round of duty, dearly beloved, brings all other virtues into action: it attains to God's image and likeness and unites us inseparably with the Holy Spirit.[35]

Leo maintained the church's invisible unity in charity by the Spirit, but he strongly emphasized the need for Christians to enact charity by caring for the poor and needy.

The peace that Christ gave to the apostles was the Spirit of peace given to those spiritual ones, which has led them to be united in one mind in faith, hope, and charity. This peace could not hold communion with those who love the things of the world, such as heathens and heretics.[36] Following Augustine, Leo identified two loves from which proceed all desires, namely, the love of God or the love of the world.[37] These loves are opposed to each other, just as the children of the world are opposed to the society of the sons of God.[38] Those who love the world must be outcast from the family of Christ.[39] On the other hand, the works of the devil are destroyed when men's hearts are recalled to the love of God and neighbor.[40] This is the proper work and "special office" of the Holy Spirit, who grants peace to the members of the church and joins "to God those whom it removes from the world."[41] For "the love of the world does not consort with the love of God," and the peacemakers are those who are "thoroughly of one mind, and fully harmonious, and are to be called sons of God and joint-heirs with Christ, because this shall be the record of the love of God and the love of our neighbor, that we shall suffer no calamities, be in fear of no offence, but all the strife of trial ended, rest in God's most perfect peace."[42] The love of God could not be perfected without the love of neighbor.[43] Christ came not only to dwell in the saints, but also to send the fire of love to kindle a greater heat. The Holy Spirit was sent at Pentecost to reveal that in the Trinity exists the unity of loving-kindness and justice.[44] The church was meant to share in this unity of justice and peace. The church has been made one because of the peace that came from the Spirit and from Christ. [45]

In Leo's thought, the church's unity in charity must be manifested through reconciliation among the members of the church, and by the distribution of alms and care of the poor and needy.[46] Sins were vanquished by mercy and charity, and without charity, there could be no virtue.[47] Those who neglected charity did so at their own peril, while those who gave alms wiped out their sins.[48]

In Leo's sacramental theology, Christians were united in the Spirit by participating in the sacraments, especially in the celebration of the Eucharist, which Leo linked in distinctive fashion to charity to the poor. Eucharistic communion was a participation in the reality of Christ's body and blood.[49] The church as the body of Christ received the flesh of the incarnate Christ in order to be transformed into the head. "For in that mystic distribution of spiritual nourishment, that which is given and taken is of such a kind that receiving the virtue of the celestial food we pass into the flesh of him, who became our flesh."[50] This offering of sacrifice was linked to the care of the poor since Christ was found among the poor. Christ, true God and true man, has distributed gifts to the church so that those who have received him in the Eucharist may then distribute gifts among the poor, for the Christian is "clothing and feeding Christ in the poor."[51] The grace of God enabled one to love what God loved, namely one's neighbor, and to love God in one's neighbor.[52] Thus, Leo declared that there is one object of our loves, God, since by loving our neighbor we love God[53] and by loving God we love our neighbor.[54] This love shines brightest in the lives of the martyrs, who died in imitation of Christ's love.[55]

Leo constructed an ecclesiology with an elevated view of papal primacy. According to Leo, Christ gave Peter as chief of the apostles principal charge of administering Christ's gifts to all nations and to all people, for from Peter, the gifts of Christ the head "flow to all members of the body: so that anyone who dared to secede from Peter's solid rock may understand that he has no part or lot in the divine mystery."[56] Christ was the founder and shepherd of the church, but Peter was the foundation upon which he built the church. Christ invited Peter into "partnership" in his "undivided unity" by naming him rock (Matt. 16:18), so "that the building of the eternal temple by the wondrous gift of God's grace might rest on Peter's solid rock: strengthening his church so surely that neither could human rashness assail it nor the gates of hell prevail against it."[57] Unlike Augustine, Leo did not see Peter primarily as a sign of the unity of the whole Christ, head and members. Instead, Leo understood the name "rock" as a share in Christ's administration of gifts to the church throughout the world. Peter's confession of faith in Matthew 16:13–16 revealed that he was destined to benefit all nations, and he was blessed by the Lord with "the solidity of power which his name also expresses."[58] The unity of the rock was a sign of the power Peter possessed from Christ, which was then passed on to his successors.

Peter had a role in the mediation of grace by virtue of his position as head of the apostles. Christ remained the one mediator and head of the body,[59] but the church was built upon Peter in order to mediate the gifts of the head. Peter's faith was the faith of the church, and the dispensation of truth was carried out by his successors.[60] The unity of the one true faith (Eph. 4:5–6), to which nothing has been added or taken away, was preserved by the church under the leadership of the bishop of Rome.[61] Further, the strength of the Christian faith was built upon the rock of Christ who declared to Peter "on this rock I will build my church, and the gates of hell shall not prevail against it" (Matt. 16:16–18).[62] When Christ breathed upon the apostles in John 20:22–23, he gave them all the Holy Spirit, but in a preeminent way, the apostle Peter was entrusted with the Lord's flock beyond the rest of the apostles by being given the keys of the kingdom.[63] All the bishops are accorded the same honor, but Peter was granted authority and headship of the apostles from Christ. The church of Rome must follow Christ's institutions.[64] The bishop of Rome was given the power to maintain the truth in the cause of peace as the successor of Peter.[65]

In the case of a dispute between bishops, the bishop of Rome must be consulted.[66] For the unity of the body of Christ makes all healthy, that is, the unity of the bond of love, but the union of the whole body required harmony among clergy. Among the blessed apostles, Peter was given a special rank, and so too his successor had a distinction of power, for "the care of the universal church should converge toward Peter's one seat, and nothing anywhere should be separated from its head."[67] By God's precept, the bishop of Rome had been tasked with watching over all the churches and offering rebuke and correction when necessary.[68] To be united as the church meant to be united through the mediation of the pope. In order to be united with Christ the head, the members had to be united with the bishop of Rome, who mediated the grace from the head.

Leo understood the church as the means of salvation for the entire world. The whole church found throughout the world must continue in love and holiness, particularly in the city of Rome, which was the citadel of the apostolic rock Peter.[69] Leo followed Augustine's view of God's providential plan for the rise of the Roman empire. However, Leo went beyond Augustine by asserting that God chose to extend the Roman empire in order to extend grace to the whole world. "The result of this unspeakable grace might be spread abroad throughout the world, God's providence made ready the Roman empire, whose growth has reached such limits that the whole multitude of nations are brought into close connection."[70]

Peter was appointed to Rome, the citadel of the Empire, so that the light of truth and the grace of Christ might spread more effectively to all nations.

> For when the twelve Apostles, after receiving through the Holy Ghost the power of speaking with all tongues, had distributed the world into parts among themselves, and undertaken to instruct it in the Gospel, the most blessed Peter,

chief of the apostolic band, was appointed to the citadel of the Roman empire, that the light of truth which was being displayed for the salvation of all the nations, might spread itself more effectively throughout the body of the world from the head itself. What nation had not representatives then living in this city; or what peoples did not know what Rome had learnt?[71]

God had chosen the city of Rome to be seat of the church and the empire in order to accomplish salvation. This was God's plan before the founding of the world. "For the saving of all through the cross of Christ was the common will and the common plan of the Father and the Son; nor could that by any means be disturbed which before eternal ages had been mercifully determined and unchangeably foreordained."[72] Christ's passion was offered for the salvation of the whole body, the church.[73] The blessings of Christ extended not only to those after, but also to those before, for "from the constitution of the world he ordained one and the same cause of salvation for all. For the grace of God, by which the whole body of the saints is ever justified, was augmented, not begun, when Christ was born: and this mystery of God's great love, wherewith the whole world is now filled, was so effectively presignified that those who believed that promise obtained no less than they, who were the actual recipients."[74] Following Augustine, Leo suggested that Christ's salvation was effective for all the members of the body who came before Christ the head, and for all that followed. Leo did not offer a theology of grace as sophisticated as Augustine's, but he seemed to suggest that God's offer of salvation had been made available to all by means of Christ and the church, regardless of whether or not it would be accepted.

Leo sought to elevate papal authority not only in the church but also in civic society. The transition from a pagan to a Christian empire had enabled Christians to participate in the socio-political world in new ways. With the instability of political powers, the bishop of Rome exercised leadership in the church and in the world. This did not mean that the pope was reducible to a political figure, however, it did recognize that the bishop of Rome played a significant role on the world stage. Leo declared that Rome was chosen by God to be the preeminent episcopacy because of Rome's relationship to the rest of the empire. Just as Rome was meant to lead the empire, so too the episcopal see of Rome was founded on the rock of Peter, the leader of the apostles. Leo went beyond the previous Latin tradition by positing the church not merely as a parallel society, but as a divinely instituted spiritual *imperium*, which must be respected and supported by any imperial administration. The church was the eternal city, but the emperor was charged with its protection. The emperor acted rightly by rooting out and deposing heretics on behalf of Catholic unity and truth.[75] The emperor served as an instrument of the divine will and embodied the traditional Roman virtues.[76] He retained the right to summon a council of bishops, over which the bishop of Rome presided. However, the imperial power must not attempt to interfere with the internal affairs of the church, for the bishop of Rome exercised this power. The emperor was the Christian prince,[77] while the pope was prince of the universal church.[78]

Further, according to Leo, the bishop of Rome was the spiritual head of the whole world through the primacy of Peter's holy see.[79] As the head of the church, the bishop of Rome was responsible for mediating the grace of God from Christ the head to the rest of the body. While the church's unity was constituted spiritually by the gift of charity among the members, the mission of the church as the agent of God's grace to the world was embodied in the person of the successor of Peter. Whatever was done rightly by Peter was done by Christ. Peter was placed over the calling of all peoples, and Peter properly reigned over all whom Christ ruled first of all.[80] This Petrine authority was passed on to each successor, with the mission to share in the partnership of Christ to administer grace to people from all nations. Thus, Leo's understanding of papal primacy added both a mediatory and missionary dimension to the church's identity since the Petrine office served as the mediator of graces to be shared by the members of the church composed of all nations.

NO SALVATION OUTSIDE OF THE CHURCH

According to Leo, Christ was the source of all salvation, and the apostle Peter was given the "principal charge" to ensure that the Gospel would go out into every land and to the end of the world.[81] In Leo's view, this meant that through Peter, the gifts of the head would flow to all members of the body, "so that anyone who dares to secede from Peter's solid rock may understand that he has no part or lot in the divine mystery."[82] As the rock upon which the church was built and by being received into partnership with Christ, "the building of the eternal temple by the wondrous gift of God's grace might rest on Peter's solid rock: strengthening his church so surely that neither could human rashness assail it nor the gates of hell prevail against it."[83] Peter played a mediatory role in the building up of the church as the temple of God, not in opposition to Christ's mediation, but in partnership with it. This was also a share in the Holy Spirit, for it was through the Spirit that the church was sanctified.

> [Through the Holy Spirit] the whole Catholic Church is sanctified, and every rational soul quickened; who is the inspirer of the faith, the teacher of knowledge, the fount of love, the seal of chastity, and the cause of all power. Let the minds of the faithful rejoice, that throughout the world one God, Father, Son, and Holy Ghost, is praised by the confession of all tongues, and that that sign of his presence, which appeared in the likeness of fire, is still perpetuated in

his work and gift. For the Spirit of truth himself makes the house of his glory shine with the brightness of his light, and will have nothing dark nor lukewarm in his temple.[84]

Salvation was found only in the Catholic Church with Peter as the rock and foundation of the temple of God. To be in the unity of the church meant to be in unity with Peter, through whom the grace of Christ was mediated. The Holy Spirit was at work in order to bring the light of truth to all the nations. Like Augustine before him, Leo granted that those just who lived before Christ could be joined to the one church, but this did not undermine the mediation of Christ and the church. Instead, all who were offered salvation were brought into the church's unity of grace under Christ the head and built upon the rock of Peter.

Leo did not address the issue of grace as Augustine did. In Augustine's mature thought, the grace of God was only given to the elect. The church remained the mediator of salvation to the world, and thus the church was the universal source of salvation. However, this did not mean that all were saved, for only those who shared in charity according to God's plan of predestination were members of the dove. In addition, Augustine argued that God gave the graces of conversion and perseverance only to the elect. Those who remained in their sins were the reprobate. Thus, in Augustine's teaching, God did not offer grace to all, nor could it be said that salvation was offered to all. The church was the universal mediator of salvation for the elect, who could be joined to the unity of the charity whether inside or outside of the visible church.

Leo did not offer a highly developed theology of grace, instead, he focused on the mediatory role of Peter and his successor in the administration of graces to the whole world. Christ was the one mediator and source of grace, but Peter was given partnership in the dispensation of graces to the church. In this capacity as head of the church and mediator of graces, the episcopal see of Peter was established in Rome in order for the pope to bring the light of Christ to all nations.

> Peter was sent to Rome as part of God's providential plan to bring salvation to the world. For when the twelve apostles, after receiving through the Holy Ghost the power of speaking with all tongues, had distributed the world into parts among themselves, and undertaken to instruct it in the Gospel, the most blessed Peter, chief of the apostolic band, was appointed to the citadel of the Roman empire, that the light of truth which was being displayed for the salvation of all the nations, might spread itself more effectively throughout the body of the world from the head itself.[85]

Although Leo did not write extensively on topics such as election and predestination, he seemed to suggest, in contradistinction to an Augustinian theology, that grace was made available to the whole body of the world from the head, that is, from Peter, who shared in the headship of Christ. For "what nation had not representatives then living in this city; or what peoples did not know what Rome had learnt?"[86] Leo certainly held that no salvation could be found outside of the church, for salvation was through the one mediator between God and humanity, Christ. However, Christ had chosen Peter to dispense his gifts to the rest of the body, so union with Christ meant union with the hierarchical structure of the church. Some could be saved outside of visible unity with the Catholic Church, both before and after the coming of Christ, but saving grace could only come from Christ and the Catholic Church so that all who were saved were joined to the one city set up on a hill.

CONCLUSION

Leo's ecclesiology was traditional in terms of the four marks of the church as one, holy, catholic, and apostolic, yet his emphasis upon the authority of the bishop of Rome helped shape the Western understanding of papal primacy. The church was guaranteed unity and apostolicity because of the successor of Peter, who enjoyed the fullness of power given by Christ to Peter over the apostles and the bishops.[87] This power was exercised in terms of doctrine, practice, and jurisdiction. Those who denied the authority and power of the bishop of Rome were cut off from the church.

> [For he denies] even the reverence that is paid to the blessed Peter himself with his proud words: for not only was the power of loosing and binding given to Peter before the others, but also to Peter more especially was entrusted the care of feeding the sheep. Yet anyone who holds that the headship must be denied to Peter, cannot really diminish his dignity: but is puffed up with the breath of his pride, and plunges himself into the lowest depth.[88]

The church's unity in charity meant unity with the successor of Peter, whose mission was to bring the Gospel to the whole world. Those who persisted in open rebellion and schism were to be excommunicated and cut off from the church. The consequence was that they no longer received the graces that came from Christ the head. They were also deprived of the sanctification of the Holy Spirit, the fount of love and the cause of power. Leo's ecclesiology differed from both Cyprian and Augustine, for the church's unity was linked directly to recognition of the authority of the bishop of Rome as the mediator of Christ's gifts and graces. This was Leo's major contribution to Latin ecclesiology, and it would shape the doctrine of papal primacy in the medieval period and in the history of Western Christianity to come.

NOTES

1. Evans, *One and Holy*, 130.
2. Leo, *Ep.* 9.3.
3. Susan Wessel, *Leo the Great and the Spiritual Rebuilding of a Universal Rome* (Leiden: Brill, 2008), 2.
4. Wessel, *Leo the Great and the Spiritual Rebuilding of a Universal Rome*, 34.
5. Augustine, *Ep.* 191.1.
6. Wessel, *Leo the Great and the Spiritual Rebuilding of a Universal Rome*, 36.
7. Bronwen Neil, *Leo the Great* (New York: Routledge, 2009), 6.
8. Neil, *Leo the Great*, 8–9.
9. Wessel, *Leo the Great and the Spiritual Rebuilding of a Universal Rome*, 4.
10. Wessel, *Leo the Great and the Spiritual Rebuilding of a Universal Rome*, 22–23.
11. Wessel, *Leo the Great and the Spiritual Rebuilding of a Universal Rome*, 19.
12. Leo, *Ep.* 10.2.
13. Leo, *Ep.* 59.3.
14. Leo, *Ep.* 59.4.
15. Leo, *Ep.* 59.4; *Serm.* 35.4.
16. Leo, *Ep.* 59.5; *Ep.* 31.2.
17. Leo, *Ep.* 88.1.
18. Leo, *Ep.* 88.2.
19. Leo, *Serm.* 30.7, citing Col. 2:8–10.
20. Leo, *Ep.* 139.4; *Ep.* 35.1.
21. Leo, *Serm.* 21.2.
22. Leo, *Serm.* 21.3.
23. Leo, *Serm.* 72.5.
24. Leo, *Serm.* 21.3.
25. Leo, *Serm.* 22.3; *Ep.* 28.2.
26. Leo, *Serm.* 23.5; Leo, *The Letters and Sermons of Leo the Great, Bishop of Rome*, trans. Charles Feltoe (NPNF 212), 375.
27. Leo, *Serm.* 22.5.
28. Leo, *Serm.* 26.3.
29. Leo, *Serm.* 26.3.
30. Leo, *Ep.* 16.4.
31. Leo, *Serm.* 77.1.
32. Leo, *Ep.* 35.1.
33. Leo, *Serm.* 75.3–5.
34. The ancient church practiced fasting on Wednesdays and Fridays; Leo, *Serm.* 12.4.
35. Leo, *Serm.* 12.4; Leo, *The Letters and Sermons of Leo the Great* (NPNF 212), 352; *Serm.* 11.4.
36. Leo, *Serm.* 26.5.
37. Leo, *Serm.* 90.3.
38. Leo, *Serm.* 95.9; PL 54.371: "amor mundi cum dei amore non congruit, nec ad societatem filiorum dei peruenit."
39. Leo, *Serm.* 26.4.
40. Leo, *Ep.* 95.2.
41. Leo, *Serm.* 26.3.
42. Leo, *Serm.* 95.9.
43. Leo, *Serm.* 12.2.
44. Leo, *Serm.* 77.1.
45. Leo, *Serm.* 50.6.
46. Leo, *Serm.* 50.6; *Serm.* 17.1; 19.3.
47. Leo, *Serm.* 74.5.
48. Leo, *Serm.* 11.3–4.
49. Leo, *Serm.* 91.3; Leo, *The Letters and Sermons of Leo the Great* (NPNF 212), 508.

50. Leo, *Ep.* 59.2. This letter suggests that infants received communion, a practice that was common in the ancient church; Leo, *The Letters and Sermons of Leo the Great* (NPNF 212), 154n385.

51. Leo, *Serm.* 91.3; Leo, *The Letters and Sermons of Leo the Great* (NPNF 212), 508; *Serm.* 9.3.

52. Leo, *Serm.* 72.5.

53. Leo, *Serm.* 95.6.

54. Leo, *Serm.* 90.3.

55. Leo, *Serm.* 85.1.

56. Leo, *Ep.* 10.1; Leo, *The Letters and Sermons of Leo the Great* (NPNF 212), 39; PL 54.633: "sed huius muneris sacramentum ita dominus ad omnium apostolorum officium pertinere voluit, ut in beatissimo petro apostolorum omnium summo, principaliter collocarit; et ab ipso quasi quodam capite, dona sua uelit in corpus omne manare, ut exsortem se mysterii intelligeret esse diuini, qui ausus fuisset a petri soliditate recedere."

57. Leo, *Ep.* 10.1; Leo, *The Letters and Sermons of Leo the Great* (NPNF 212), 39; PL 54.633–34: "hunc enim in consortium indiuiduae unitatis assumptum, id quod ipse erat, uoluit nominari, dicendo: *tu es petrus, et super hanc petram aedificabo ecclesiam meam*; ut aeterni templi aedificatio, mirabili munere gratiae dei, in petri soliditate consisteret; hac ecclesiam suam firmitate corroborans, ut illam nec humana temeritas posset appetere, nec portae contra illam inferi praeualerent."

58. Leo, *Ep.* 28.5; Leo, *The Letters and Sermons of Leo the Great* (NPNF 212), 106; 33.1; 119.2; *Serm.* 3.2; 62.2.

59. Leo, *Ep.* 28.3; 35.3; 108.2; 124.2–6; *Serm.* 21.2; 31.1; 63.2.

60. Leo, *Serm.* 3.2–3; *Serm.* 51.1–2.

61. Leo, *Serm.* 24.6.

62. Leo, *Serm.* 62.2; 24.6.

63. Leo, *Serm.* 73.2.

64. Leo, *Ep.* 9.1.

65. Leo, *Ep.* 43.1.

66. Leo, *Ep.* 14.12.

67. Leo, *Ep.* 14.12.

68. Leo, *Ep.* 16.1.

69. Leo, *Serm.* 8.4.

70. Leo, *Serm.* 82.2; Leo, *The Letters and Sermons of Leo the Great* (NPNF 212), 493.

71. Leo, *Serm.* 82.3; Leo, *The Letters and Sermons of Leo the Great* (NPNF 212), 493.

72. Leo, *Serm.* 58.4.

73. Leo, *Serm.* 58.5.

74. Leo, *Serm.* 23.4; Leo, *The Letters and Sermons of Leo the Great* (NPNF 212), 375.

75. Evans, *One and Holy*, 131.

76. Evans, *One and Holy*, 133.

77. Leo, *Ep.* 45.2.

78. Leo, *Ep.* 14.12.

79. Leo, *Serm.* 82.1.

80. Neil, *Leo the Great*, 41.

81. Leo, *Ep.* 10.1.

82. Leo, *Ep.* 10.1.

83. Leo, *Ep.* 10.1.

84. Leo, *Serm.* 76.5.

85. Leo, *Serm.* 82.3.

86. Leo, *Serm.* 82.3.

87. Leo, *Serm.* 14.1; 10.2.

88. Leo, *Ep.* 10.2.

Conclusion

The Second Vatican Council's Dogmatic Constitution on the Church *Lumen Gentium*, promulgated in November 1964, begins by declaring that "Christ is the light of the nations" and the head of his body, the church.[1] The fathers of the council use Biblical images in order to describe the church as a mystery with visible and invisible aspects. These aspects of the church are distinct yet inseparable, for there is only one church, just as there is one Spirit, one body, and one mediator.

> The one mediator, Christ, established and constantly sustains here on earth his holy church, the community of faith, hope and charity, as a visible structure through which he communicates truth and grace to everyone. But, the society equipped with hierarchical structures and the mystical body of Christ, the visible society and the spiritual community, the earthly church and the church endowed with heavenly riches, are not to be thought of as two realities. On the contrary, they form one complex reality comprising a human and divine element.[2]

This conciliar teaching captured an essential feature of Latin patristic ecclesiology: the church is a visible, empirical community that mediates grace and truth. At the same time, it is an invisible, spiritual body united in charity by the Holy Spirit. This is a distinction without separation, for there is only one complex reality, one church with visible and invisible dimensions. According to the Latin fathers, the visible serves as a means for the invisible. The Holy Spirit works through the sacraments in order to mediate grace and charity. Yet the Spirit is not limited by material things. The church is a visible body united in the invisible bond of charity. God works through the visible celebrations of the sacraments, but God is not limited by them.

In *Lumen Gentium* 8, the council fathers affirm the four traditional marks of the church found in early Latin ecclesiology.

> This is the unique church of Christ which in the Creed we profess to be one, holy, catholic, and apostolic. . . . This church, constituted and organized as a society in the present world, subsists in the Catholic Church. . . . Nevertheless, many elements of sanctification and of truth are found outside its visible confines. Since these are gifts belonging to the church of Christ, they are forces impelling towards Catholic unity.[3]

The Latin fathers offered distinctive views of the church's four marks. They recognized the invisible work of Christ and the Spirit beyond the visible bounds of the church, yet they understood that the gift of charity was given in order to draw all into the one unity of charity, the very same charity mediated by the sacraments of the Catholic Church. Thus, the Latin fathers could assert that outside of the one church, there was no salvation, for those who were saved were joined to the invisible union of charity. Some who were outside the visible community could be joined to this church invisibly by the power and work of the Spirit. However, this did not render the visible, empirical church ineffective or incidental to salvation. For those who were saved enjoyed the gifts that belonged to the one church of Christ.

For the Latin fathers, the church was necessary for salvation, but this did not necessarily require participation in the rituals of the empirical community. For instance, the martyrs were baptized by blood. They were joined to the same union of charity mediated by the baptismal ritual of the cleansing with water and the impositions of hands. Thus, the early Latin fathers offered a theological foundation upon which to uphold the mediation of Christ and the church while maintaining that people from all nations could be brought into the saving light of Christ.

THE FOUR MARKS OF THE CHURCH

Tertullian of Carthage, the earliest Latin theologian whose writings survive, privileged the church's spiritual unity over hierarchical unity. The church's unity in charity was constituted by the union of the whole Christ, head and members, as one body. The Holy Spirit was sent upon the whole church to unite the members in charity by means of the sacraments. Baptism provided entrance into the universal priesthood of believers. Tertullian upheld the mediatory role of the clergy in the preservation of truth and the administration of the sacraments by virtue of apostolic succession. The church was one and holy because of the charity of the Spirit. It was catholic and apostolic because of continuity in doctrine, practice, and apostolic lineage.

Tertullian's ecclesiology was marked by a kind of rigorism that did not permit anyone who committed serious sins to be readmitted to the fellowship of the church so as to preserve the holiness of the church. Those guilty of grave sins such as idolatry, adultery, fornication, and murder should ask forgiveness from God, beg for intercessory prayers, and hope for God's mercy, but they were not permitted to participate in the eucharistic communion of the church. In Tertullian's view, the church had to be preserved from the stain and impurity of sin. This meant permanent exclusion of sinners.

Tertullian based this claim on a strong association of the church with the Triune God. Where Christ and the Holy Spirit are, there is the church, and there is no room for evil and sin. Further, in his understanding of apostolic authority, the clergy did not possess the power to forgive serious sins. The clergy were entrusted with administering the sacraments and maintaining unity in terms of doctrine and practice. They were not able to forgive sins by virtue of their episcopal authority, for the power to forgive sins belonged to the spiritual ones, that is, to the members of Christ's body united in charity. Yet not even the spiritual ones could forgive grave sins, and those who committed such monstrosities as adultery and fornication had to be given over to the destruction of the flesh (1 Cor. 5:5). Grave sin was a kind of self-destruction, and in Tertullian's view, it was impossible for these persons to be restored to the fellowship of the church. Their only hope was God's mercy at the final judgment. The chaff had to be separated from the wheat, for there was no room for evil among the spiritual ones. Thus, Tertullian developed a rigorist, exclusivist ecclesiology that demanded the removal of sinners from the church in order to maintain its unity and holiness.

Against this kind of rigorism, Cyprian of Carthage advocated a more moderate approach that enabled sinners to be reconciled to the church after performing penance, according to the provisions of the local bishop. Cyprian inherited the early Christian understanding of idolatry as a contagion or pollution. Cyprian initially did not permit readmission of the lapsed in order to protect against a laxist policy. However, after meeting with and listening to his fellow bishops in the episcopal college, Cyprian decided that sinners should be granted the opportunity to be readmitted to the community and to eucharistic fellowship. To support this claim, Cyprian argued that Christ gave the Holy Spirit to Peter and the apostles along with the power to forgive sins (John 20:22–23). Peter represented the unity of the apostles, and each bishop, as a successor of the apostles, was offered a participation in this unity. It was only by sharing in this unity that the bishop had the power to sanctify with the Holy Spirit. Those who cut themselves off from this unity were no longer able to sanctify since they could not give what they had not received.

Cyprian moved away from the rigorist position while also avoiding a laxist policy. His argument for the practice of reconciling sinners was based upon an ecclesiology in which the bishops were granted the power to sanctify by the Holy Spirit, in virtue of their unity with the episcopal college. Schismatics lacked effective baptism and other sacraments because they lacked the Holy Spirit. The church could readmit penitents after the proper process of purification and the imposition of hands by the bishop, thereby restoring the sinner to communion with the church in charity. If, however, the bishop was not in union with the universal worldwide episcopacy, he and his congregation lacked the Holy Spirit. The church was one, holy, catholic, and apostolic by virtue of the bishop's union with the episcopal college as a sign of the union shared by Peter and the apostles.

Like Cyprian, Augustine sought ways to readmit the lapsed into the communion of the church. However, he did so by constructing a strikingly different ecclesiology. Augustine held, as Tertullian did, that the Holy Spirit belonged to the whole church as the body of Christ. When Christ conferred the power of the Spirit upon Peter and the apostles in John 20:22–23, he granted it to the entire communion of saints united in charity. The bishops did not have special possession of the Spirit by virtue of their unity with the episcopal college. They administered the sacraments, but the power and efficacy of the sacraments came from Christ and the Spirit. Anyone who had been ordained validly received the ability to celebrate the sacraments. Cyprian and the Donatists were both wrong on this account, but Cyprian prized unity over division, so he could be pardoned for his theological error. The Donatists had the power to celebrate the sacraments, but when they did so in a state of schism, they did not enjoy the fruits of the sacraments. Instead, they heaped punishment upon themselves. Nevertheless, their sacraments were efficacious because of the power of Christ. This applied not only to baptism but to the other sacraments, such as reconciliation.

Augustine's understanding of the sacrament of reconciliation further reveals how far he had diverged from Cyprian's view of the necessary mediation of the bishop to maintain the church's unity. Like Tertullian, Augustine held that the charity that forgave sins belonged to the whole Christ, head and members. When the penitent was forgiven, it was not due to the power conferred upon the bishop due to his unity with the episcopacy, rather, it was because of the charity of the saints. Whether or not the bishop was in unity with his colleagues, he could confer the sacrament of reconciliation, and the penitent would be forgiven because of the forgiveness offered by the whole Christ. Augustine affirmed apostolic succession as a sign of the union of the whole church, whose unity in charity was mediated by the sacraments of the visible, worldwide Catholic Church. However, Augustine denied Cyprian's understanding of the unity of the episcopal college as necessary for the efficacy of the sacraments. On the contrary, he asserted against Cyprian and the Donatists that properly ordained bishops could celebrate the sacraments, no matter what their moral status or union with the episcopal college. While

Cyprian rightly prized unity and attempted to bring back sinners into the fold, he wrongly privileged the episcopal college as the basis for the unity of the church and the efficacy of the sacraments. Augustine's teaching provided the foundation for a sacramental theology in which the sacraments confer grace by virtue of their own operation, or as it was later expressed, *ex opere operato*.

In contradistinction to Tertullian's theology, Augustine asserted that the church's holiness was not harmed by the presence of sinners in her midst. To be sure, Augustine insisted that those who committed serious sins had to undergo reconciliation prior to participation in the eucharistic sacrifice. Cyprian and other North African bishops were right to provide opportunities for sinners to be readmitted to the church by penitential practices. Nevertheless, Augustine recognized that there were some who received the sacraments unworthily. All the members of the church were fallen and sinful, and some may fall into serious sin even after baptism and reconciliation. Chaff was found among the wheat in the church. According to Augustine, the wheat and chaff would only be separated at the end time, when the spotless bride would be revealed in glory. Until then, the church remained a mixed body of good and wicked, elect and reprobate. The presence of sinners did not harm the holiness of the church, for the unity of the saints in charity could tolerate any scandal. Those who received the sacraments while remaining unrepentant did so to their own detriment. As a mixed body, the church had to undergo purification until the final eschatological separation. This meant bearing with sinners rather than expelling them from the community. By Augustine's own exhortation, Christians were obligated to rebuke and to correct one another if a member should fall into sin. This would enable the sinner to begin on the proper path to reconciliation with the church. During the church's earthly pilgrimage, the saints were purified and conformed to the patience of God, while the wicked were given the opportunity to convert.

Augustine offers an inclusive ecclesiology, wherein the visible church mediates charity and the grace of God in order to transform sinners into saints. While all of the members of the church are sinners, they are purified by participating in a community defined by the two-fold love of God and neighbor. The presence of the wicked does not harm the church's unity in love, for love covers a multitude of sins (1 Pet. 4:8). Even serious sinners can be reconciled, not because of episcopal unity and authority (although this was a necessary but not sufficient condition for reconciliation), but precisely because of the forgiveness offered by the saints united in charity. After participating in the sacrament of reconciliation, penitents could be readmitted to eucharistic communion.

Augustine's ecclesiology is also notable for its distinctive understanding of the church's mediation of salvation and holiness. In Augustine's view, there is only one way of salvation, through Christ and his church, the Catholic Church. However, Augustine posited that the Holy Spirit could operate beyond the Catholic Church's visible bounds in order to bring some into the one union of charity. Catechumens who were martyred received baptism by blood, and those who died while seeking the Spirit could be joined to charity in the future. Further, Augustine suggested that the holy ones of the Old Testament were members of the body of Christ. The church on earth began with Abel, who offered a pleasing sacrifice to God. Abraham was saved by his faith. All of the just were saved by virtue of Christ's saving power, which could be applied by means of the Old Testament sacraments, such as circumcision. Thus, according to Augustine, there is no salvation outside of the church, for the church extends to all who are united in charity to the one body of Christ, whether they are inside or outside of the visible Catholic Church.

Leo the Great followed the main lines of Augustine's theology of the church, but his understanding of the church as Catholic and apostolic privileged the bishop of Rome as the successor of Peter. By the time of Leo's election as the bishop of Rome, Christianity had become the dominant religion of the empire. For some, this explained why the empire was in ruins. Rome had been ravaged by the Goths, Vandals, and barbarians, and there was political turmoil among the Roman emperors. There was also division among Christians in the East and West over doctrine, specifically Christology. Leo took this as an opportunity to expand papal authority, both in relation to Roman society and to the church as a whole. Leo relied upon Christ's declaration of Peter as the rock in Matthew 16 as evidence of Peter's singular participation in the salvific work of Christ. As the rock, Peter was granted a partnership in the mediation of grace from Christ the head. This meant that the bishop of Rome, as the successor of Peter, played a mediatory role in the dispensation of grace to the whole church. The pope exercised this mediation by settling doctrinal disputes, exerting jurisdictional authority, and bringing the Gospel to all nations. Thus, unity with the church meant submission to the authority of the Roman bishop.

Leo sought to bring the pope to prominence in a society that had been Christianized but was politically unstable. To the imperial authorities, Leo entrusted the protection and preservation of the church as a divine mandate. They were empowered to guard the church and to purify it of heretics, with the use of force if necessary. However, the emperor had to respect the authority of the bishop of Rome, who remained the head of the church. While the Roman emperor was the prince, the bishop of Rome was the spiritual head of the whole world and the whole city of God. Leo was responsible for an elevated doctrine of papal primacy, which was forged in a time of changing dynamics between church and state. Leo established the bishop of Rome as a leader in the church and in society for the good of the world and for the conversion of all nations to the one true faith. There was no salvation outside of the one Catholic Church, united around the authority of the bishop of Rome.

ONE CHURCH, VISIBLE AND INVISIBLE

Ecclesiology in the Latin West took shape over the course of several centuries in different contexts. The church was defined according to four marks as one, holy, catholic, and apostolic, outside of which there was no salvation. The Latin fathers all arrived at these conclusions, but they argued for them in different ways. By the fifth century, there emerged an emphasis upon union with the bishop of Rome not only in terms of doctrine, sacraments, and apostolic lineage (Tertullian and Augustine), but also in terms of the unique mediation of grace, whether by virtue of a local bishop's union with the episcopal college symbolized by Peter's union with the apostles (Cyprian), or due to the pope's distinctive role in the mediation of grace to the whole church as the successor of Peter (Leo).

Further, the church's unity in charity meant something different for each one of these Latin fathers. All agreed that there was only one church, with visible and invisible aspects that could be distinguished yet not separated. As such, there could be many elements of sanctification and truth found outside of the visible, empirical community, but the gift of charity belonged to the one church by the power of the Holy Spirit, who would bring all into the union of the one Christ, head and members.

In the development of Latin ecclesiology over the first five centuries of Christianity, there was a discernible trajectory away from an exclusive, rigoristic ecclesiology to a more inclusive view of church membership, due in large part to the work of Cyprian and Augustine. The church has room for saints and sinners, for every saint is a sinner, and every sinner can become a saint. There remains a proper order for participation in the sacraments, culminating with the eucharistic fellowship of the church. Yet even those guilty of grave sins could be readmitted to the unity of the church, for charity covers a multitude of sins and can bear any scandal due to sin. The Augustinian picture of the church that emerged in the fifth century was not one of an exclusive, elitist club reserved solely for the sinless. Instead, the church was a community of imperfect members, undergoing the slow process of growth, transformation, and conformation to Christ by participation in the sacraments and by practices such as prayer, fasting, and almsgiving. The church was the place for healing by sharing in the two-fold love of God and neighbor, which is charity.[4] This spiritual transformation occurred by participation in the empirical community, a community bound in love. This is what should distinguish Christians from those groups around them. Christians should be known by their love. The Holy Spirit works not to separate or to divide, but to unite all in the one bond of charity shared among the members of the one Christ. Therefore, what God has joined together let no one put asunder.

NOTES

1. LG 1; 7.
2. LG 8.
3. LG 8.
4. Augustine, *Serm.* 179.4.

Bibliography

PRIMARY SOURCE TRANSLATIONS

Augustine of Hippo. *Answer to Faustus*. Translated by Roland Teske. WSA I/20.
———. *The City of God*. Translated by William Babcock. WSA I/7.
———. *Confessions*. Translated by Maria Boulding. WSA I/1.
———. *The Donatist Controversy I*. Translated by Maureen Tilley. WSA I/21.
———. *Expositions of the Psalms 1–32*. Translated by Maria Boulding. WSA III/15.
———. *Expositions of the Psalms 51–72*. Translated by Maria Boulding. WSA III/17.
———. *Homilies on First John*. Translated by Boniface Ramsey. WSA III/13.
———. *Instructing Beginners in Faith*. Translated by Raymond Canning. New York: New City Press, 2006.
Cyprian of Carthage. *On the Church: Select Treatises*. Translated by Allen Brent. Crestwood: St. Vladimir's Seminary Press, 2006.
Leo. *The Letters and Sermons of Leo the Great, Bishop of Rome*. Translated by Charles Feltoe. NPNF 212.
Tertullian. *On Modesty*. Translated by S. Thelwall. In *The Fathers of the Third Century*. Edited by A. Cleveland Coxe. ANF 4.

SELECT SECONDARY SOURCES

Barnes, Timothy. *Tertullian: A Historical and Literary Study*. Oxford: Oxford University Press, 1985.
Bray, Gerald. *Holiness and the Will of God: Perspectives on the Theology of Tertullian*. London: Marshall, Morgan, and Scott, 1979.
Brent, Allen. *Cyprian and Roman Carthage*. New York: Cambridge, 2010.
Burns, J. Patout. *Cyprian the Bishop*. London: Routledge, 2002.
———. "Establishing Unity in Diversity." *Perspectives in Religious Studies* 32:4 (2005): 381–99.
Burns, J. Patout, Robin M. Jensen, et al. *Christianity in Roman Africa: The Development of Its Practices and Beliefs*. Grand Rapids: Eerdmans, 2014.
Cameron, Michael. *Christ Meets Me Everywhere*. New York: Oxford University Press, 2012.
———. "Transfiguration: Christology and the Roots of Figurative Exegesis in St. Augustine." *Studia Patristica* 33 (1997): 40–47.

Chadwick, Henry. *The Church in Ancient Society: From Galilee to Gregory the Great.* New York: Oxford University Press, 2001.
Cavadini, John. "Ideology and Solidarity in Augustine's *City of God.*" In *Augustine's* City of God: *A Critical Guide*, edited by James Wetzel, 93–110. New York: Cambridge University Press, 2012.
Decret, Francois. *Early Christianity in North Africa.* Translated by Edward L. Smither. Eugene: Cascade, 2009.
Dulles, Avery and Patrick Granfield. *The Church: A Bibliography.* Wilmington: Michael Glazier, 1985.
Dunn, Geoffrey D. "Augustine's Use of the Pauline Portrayal of Peter in Galatians 2." *Augustinian Studies* 46:1 (2015): 23–42.
———. *Cyprian and the Bishops of Rome: Questions of Papal Primacy in the Early Church.* Strathfield, NSW: St Pauls, 2017.
———. "Heresy and Schism According to Cyprian of Carthage." *Journal of Theological Studies* 55: 2 (2004): 551–74.
———. *Tertullian.* New York: Routledge, 2004.
———. *Tertullian's Aduersus Iudaeos: A Rhetorical Analysis.* Patristic Monograph 19. Washington, DC: Catholic University of America Press, 2008.
Eno, Robert. *Teaching Authority in the Early Church.* Wilmington: Michael Glazier, 1984.
Evans, G. R. "The Church in the Early Christian Centuries: Ecclesiological Consolidation." In *The Routledge Companion to the Christian Church*, edited by Gerard Mannion and Lewis S. Mudge, 28–47. New York: Routledge, 2007.
Evans, Robert. *One and Holy: The Church in Latin Patristic Thought.* London: S.P.C.K., 1972.
Ferguson, Everett. "Community and Worship." In *The Routledge Companion to Early Christian Thought*, edited by D. Jeffrey Bingham, 313–30. New York: Routledge, 2010.
Fiedrowicz, Michael. *Psalmus vox totius Christi: Studien zu Augustins 'Enarrationes in Psalmos'.* Freiburg: Herder, 1997.
Gaumer, Matthew A. *Augustine's Cyprian: Authority in Roman Africa.* Leiden: Brill, 2016.
Gil-Tamayo, J.A. *Cyprian: Obras completas.* Madrid: BAC, 2013.
Hall, Stuart G. "The Early Idea of the Church." In *The First Christian Theologians: An Introduction to Theology in the Early Church*, edited by G. R. Evans, 41–57. Malden: Blackwell, 2004.
Harmless, William. *Augustine and the Catechumenate.* Collegeville: Liturgical Press, 1995.
Heffernan, Thomas J. *The Passion of Perpetua and Felicity.* Oxford: Oxford University Press, 2012.
Hinson, E. Glenn. *Understandings of the Church.* In *Sources of Early Christian Thought*, edited by William G. Rusch. Philadelphia: Fortress Press, 1986.
Lander, Shira. *Ritual Sites and Religious Rivalries in Late Roman North Africa.* Cambridge: Cambridge University Press, 2016.
Lee, James K. *Augustine and the Mystery of the Church.* Minneapolis: Fortress Press, 2017.
Meconi, David. *The One Christ: St. Augustine's Theology of Deification.* Washington, DC: Catholic University of America Press, 2013.
Merdinger, Jane. "Roman North Africa." In *Early Christianity in Contexts: An Exploration across Cultures and Continents*, edited by William Tabbernee, 223–60. Grand Rapids: Baker Academic, 2014.
Neil, Bronwen. *Leo the Great.* New York: Routledge, 2009.
Oden, Thomas. *Early Libyan Christianity: Uncovering a North African Tradition.* Downers Grove: Intervarsity Press, 2011.
Osborn, Eric. *Tertullian: First Theologian of the West.* New York: Cambridge University Press, 1997.
Papandrea, James. *The Trinitarian Theology of Novatian of Rome: A Study in Third-Century Orthodoxy.* Lewiston: Edwin Mellen Press, 2008.
Potthoff, Stephen E. *The Afterlife in Early Christian Carthage: Near-Death Experience, Ancestor Cult, and the Archaeology of Paradise.* New York: Routledge, 2017.
Rankin, David. *Tertullian and the Church.* Cambridge: Cambridge University Press, 1995.

Rebillard, Éric. *Christians and Their Many Identities in Late Antiquity, North Africa, 200–450 CE*. Ithaca: Cornell University Press, 2012.

Root, Michael. "Augustine on the Church." In *T&T Clark Companion to Augustine and Modern Theology*, edited by C. C. Pecknold and T. Toom, 54–74. New York: Bloomsbury T&T Clark, 2013.

Sage, Michael. *Cyprian*. Cambridge, MA: The Philadelphia Patristic Foundation, 1975.

Sebastian, J. Jayakiran. *"baptisma unum in ecclesia sancta": A Theological Appraisal of the Baptismal Controversy in the Work and Writings of Cyprian of Carthage*. Hamburg: Lottbeck Jensen, 1997.

Tabbernee, William. *Fake Prophecy and Polluted Sacraments: Ecclesiastical and Imperial Reactions to Montanism*. Leiden: Brill, 2007.

———. *Prophets and Gravestones: An Imaginative History of Montanists and Other Early Christians*. Peabody: Hendrickson Publishers, 2009.

Trevett, Christine. *Montanism: Gender, Authority and the New Prophecy*. Cambridge: Cambridge University Press, 1996.

Vranic, Vasilije. "Augustine and the Donatist Claims to Cyprianic Ecclesiological Legacy." *Philotheos* 7 (2007): 208–221.

Wessel, Susan. *Leo the Great and the Spiritual Rebuilding of a Universal Rome*. Leiden: Brill, 2008.

Whitehouse, John. "The Scholarship of the Donatist Controversy." In *The Donatist Schism: Controversy and Contexts*, edited by Richard Miles, 34–53. Liverpool: Liverpool University Press, 2016.

Wilhite, David. *Ancient African Christianity: An Introduction to a Unique Context and Tradition*. New York: Routledge, 2017.

———. *Tertullian the African: An Anthropological Reading of Tertullian's Context and Identities*. Berlin: Walter De Gruyter, 2007.

Wilken, Robert Louis. *The Christians as the Romans Saw Them*. New Haven: Yale University Press, 1984.

———. *The First Thousand Years: A Global History of Christianity*. New Haven: Yale University Press, 2012.

———. *Liberty in the Things of God: The Christian Origins of Religious Freedom*. New Haven: Yale University Press, 2019.

Index

Abel, 31, 73, 77, 79, 88n165, 112
Abraham, 73
Adam and Eve, 27, 46, 67, 69, 73, 79, 80, 95
Adeodatus, 61
almsgiving, 6, 10, 29, 33, 47, 63, 65, 78, 97, 113
Ambrose, 61–62
anointing, 18, 63, 69
apostles, 30, 51, 74, 98–99; apostolic succession, 21, 29–31, 41, 46, 50, 54, 63, 66, 99, 109
Aristotle, 61
Attila the Hun, 92
Augustine, 27, 47, 52, 59–83, 92–93, 102; *Against Faustus*, 68, 69; *Answer to the Letter of Parmenian*, 71; *Answer to the Writings of Petilian*, 71; *City of God*, 6, 62, 79; *Confessions*, 62; *On Baptism*, 72, 75, 77; *On Genesis Against the Manichees*, 67; *Teaching Christianity*, 67; *To Simplician*, 80
Aurelius, 92

Babylon (earthly city), 77, 78

Caecilian, 60, 82
Caelestine, 92
Cain, 79
charity, 5–10, 21, 28, 29, 31, 32, 46, 50–54, 64–65, 67–82, 97–98, 107–108

Christ, 7, 21, 26, 30, 32, 46–47, 64–66, 72, 93, 95–96, 98, 100, 102; Incarnation, 19, 27; mediator, 10, 66, 81, 101, 108; head of the church, 9, 50, 71, 76–79
Church: as ark, 68–69; body of Christ, 4–5, 8, 21, 26, 47, 67–70, 76, 95–96, 98; as body (mixed), 68–70, 76; as bride, 27, 52, 70; Catholic Church, 8, 64, 66, 69, 73, 81, 101–102; As city of God, 28, 77–79, 100; communion of sacraments, 53, 66, 69–70, 79–80; communion of saints, 7–8, 32, 64, 69, 75; elect, 68–69, 80, 102; as fellowship, 5, 8, 78; four marks of (one, holy, catholic, apostolic), 3, 21, 29, 32, 50–51, 72, 103, 108–113; Jerusalem, 20, 60–78; as mother, 25, 26, 50–52, 72; as sacrifice, 20, 79; temple, 25, 70
Cicero, 61
clergy, 2, 5, 16, 21, 33, 42–45, 49, 60, 65, 67; bishop, 17, 21, 31, 41, 46, 49, 51, 53, 63–66, 93–95, 99; deacon, 21, 47–49; presbyter (priest), 21, 31, 47, 49, 66, 94
confessors, 42
Constantine, 59–60
Cornelius, 44
councils: African, 5, 43–44; Chalcedon, 93; Vatican II, 107
Cyprian, 41–54, 59, 71–72; *Letter* 33, 51; *On the Lapsed*, 43; *On the Unity of the*

Church, 3, 50

Decius, 2, 42–43
demons, 17, 45
devil (Satan), 19, 80, 97; serpent in Genesis, 28
Diocletian, 60
Donatists, 7, 60, 62, 72

Edict of Milan, 6, 59
Enoch, 31, 73
episcopal college, 6, 31, 34, 41, 46, 52, 71, 81
Esau, 28, 72, 80
Eutyches, 92–93, 96

Fabian, 43–44
Faustus, 61, 68
Felicissimus, 43
forgiveness of sins, 7, 20, 26, 29, 48–49, 65, 67, 75

Gallus, 48
Goths, 6, 9, 62
grace, 10, 52, 66, 79–81, 98, 100, 102, 107

hope, 69, 75, 77, 81

Ishmael, 72

Jacob, 28, 72, 80
Jerome, 14
Judaism, 31; Jews in North Africa, 23, 31–32
Julian of Eclanum, 62

laity, 25, 28–29, 49, 53, 65
Leo, 91–103; *Tome*, 93
libellus, 5, 43–44
Lumen Gentium, 107–108

Majorinus, 60
Manichaeism, 62, 92
Marius Victorinus, 62
martyrdom, 4, 18–19, 25, 47, 73; *The Acts of the Scillitans*, 15; *The Passion of Perpetua and Felicity*, 15–16; martyrs as confessors, 20
Maximus, 45, 93

mercy, 32, 97, 98, 109
miracles, 21, 30
Monica, 61
Montanism, 13, 15, 23–24

New Prophecy. *See* Montanism
Novatian, 44

Optatus, 69, 71, 83
Osborn, Eric, 39n194

Paul, 24
Patricius, 61
Pelagius, 62, 92; Pelagianism, 92
Pentecost, 97
Peter, 6, 48, 72, 81, 98–99, 102; as head of apostles, 46, 98, 101; confession of faith, 98; rock, 30, 98, 100, 102; successor as bishop of Rome (pope), 74, 101
Plotinus, 61–62
Pontius, 42, 45; *Life of Cyprian*, 42
Porphyry, 2, 61
Predestination, 75, 76
priesthood of believers, 21, 63, 66, 108
prophecy, 28–29, 31

religion, 1, 9; Punic, 4, 16, 22
reprobate, 68, 80
Rome, 1, 9, 31, 62, 91, 93–94; Roman Empire, 6, 14, 59
rule of faith (*regula fidei*), 22, 30

sacraments of: baptism, 18, 20–21, 25–26, 28, 41, 44–46, 51–52, 63–64, 67, 69, 71–74, 81, 95, 108; Eucharist, 8, 19, 21, 43, 46–47, 51, 53, 64–65, 78, 80, 98; reconciliation, 20, 43–44, 47, 48, 64–65, 78, 97
sacrifices: Christian, 19, 23, 28, 46–47, 53, 77, 79–80, 98; Jewish, 31; Pagan, 1, 16–17, 22–23, 42–43, 51, 60
salvation, 3, 18, 31–32, 47, 52–53, 64, 66, 73, 75, 80–81, 96, 99–100, 102
scripture: Acts, 30, 48, 77, 78; 1 Cor., 27–29, 73, 109; 2 Cor., 27; Eph., 26, 50, 67–68, 70, 99; Gal., 65; Gen., 28, 67, 69, 95; Isa., 26; John, 6, 26, 41, 46, 50, 71, 74, 97, 99, 109–110; 1 John, 29;

Matt., 9, 20, 26–27, 30, 43, 50, 64, 68, 71, 98–99, 112; 1 Pet., 64, 111; Song of Sol., 50, 74–75; Rev., 20; Rom., 7, 66, 68, 71, 75, 80; 2 Tim., 69

Septimus Severus, 15

sin: adultery, 19, 20, 27, 29, 33, 34n9, 48, 49, 65, 70, 109; apostasy, 2, 4, 5, 13, 15, 20, 43, 46, 48, 49, 51, 60; fornication, 21, 27, 65; idolatry, 4, 17–19, 22, 27, 33, 45, 51, 65; grave sins, 20, 21, 26, 32, 48, 82; minor sins, 65; murder, 4, 19, 20, 65

Sixtus, 92

Spirit (Holy), 18, 20, 25–28, 45, 49, 50, 52, 64–66, 68–69, 96–97; gifts of, 21, 28–29, 64, 75–76, 78

Stephen, Pope, 6, 52

Tertullian, 13–34, 59; *Apology*, 19; *Against the Jews*, 25, 28; *Against Praxeas*, 50; *On Baptism*, 26; *On Modesty,*, 20, 26; *On Monogamy*, 27; *On Patience*, 29; *On Penance*, 20, 26; *On Prayer*, 19, 26; *Prescript Against the Heretics*, 30; *To the Martyrs*, 20, 25; *To the Nations*, 24; *To Scapula*, 20, 24

Thagaste, 61

Theodosius, 59, 92

Traditor, 60–61

Trinity, 18, 25–26, 45, 50, 96–97

Tyconius, 68

Valentinian III, 92

Valerian, 44–45

Valerius, 62

Vandals, 60, 92–93

worship, 1–2, 15, 24, 42, 45, 79–80

About the Author

James K. Lee is Associate Professor of the History of Early Christianity in the Perkins School of Theology at Southern Methodist University in Dallas, TX. He is the author of *Augustine and the Mystery of the Church* (Minneapolis: Fortress Press, 2017).

www.ingramcontent.com/pod-product-compliance
Lightning Source LLC
Chambersburg PA
CBHW050910300426
44111CB00010B/1461